S0-ASG-444

A "Digging Deeper" Study Guide
Book "A"

Ancient Civilizations & The Bible

Creation to Jesus Christ

by Diana Waring

Original illustrations by Isaac Waring

"And He has made from one blood every nation of men to dwell on all the face of the earth, and has determined their preappointed times and the boundaries of their habitation, so that they should seek the Lord..."

Acts 17:26-27

Special Thanks to all those who helped make this project happen:

- all the librarians at Grace Balloch Memorial Library, especially Kathy who never said, "Impossible";

- my friends who read the manuscript and gave enthusiastic reviews and helpful suggestions - Maxine, Heather, Bernie, and Jane;

- all the homeschoolers who requested this book, and then told us what they needed;

- Steve, who gave us a crash course in page lay-out and design;

- Jeff, who willingly took on the "clean up" of our manuscript;

- our Advisory Council who prayed us through;

- and my children, Isaac (my illustrator par excellence), Michael (the chef extraordinaire) and Melody (the cheerful one who keeps us going.)

As always, this project was the result of team-work. It would **never** have happened without my wise, patient, and generous husband, Bill.

copyright 1997 by Diana Waring

All rights reserved. No part of this book may be reproduced or transmitted in any form or by any means - graphic, electronic or mechanical, including photocopying or any information or retrieval system without written permission from the author, except for brief quotations quoted in a review.

Table of Contents

Introduction

Welcome to *Ancient Civilizations & The Bible:*
A "Digging Deeper" Study Guide Book "A" - Creation to Jesus Christ.

It is our hope and prayer that this in-depth look at human history from Creation - the beginning of history - to Jesus Christ - the centerpiece of history - will help you to:

• trust God's faithfulness;
• obey Him in your own life;
• view other cultures and peoples from His perspective;
• get a glimpse of God's sovereignty in history;
• understand the importance of **worldviews** in interpreting history;
• gain a solid foundation in **apologetics** using the Bible as literal history;
• comprehend the relevance of ancient times to today's headlines;
• have a critical and complete understanding of each of these cultures through its **Art, Science, Literature, Geography, Music, Warfare, Agriculture, Religion, Family Life, Government, Economics, Architecture, Communications, and History**, and in understanding its impact on other cultures;
• learn how to approach, appreciate and apply the study of history.

*Whether you are structured or flexible, a user of textbooks or unit studies, just beginning homeschooling or experienced, **Ancient Civilizations and the Bible** will work for you! Keep in mind that this study guide includes:*

• Twelve units - advancing chronologically;
• A cycle approach through all four learning styles **for each unit**;
• Objectives listed at the beginning **of each unit**;
• Several subject areas covered **in each unit** might include -

History	Bible	Geography	Literature
Art/Crafts	Science/Math	Music	Drama
Cooking	Poetry	Architecture	Creative Writing

• Multi-grade approach which makes this usable for the entire family! Activities included are designed to challenge the mental levels of fourth grade through high school. Depending on the age of your students, you will possibly need to add phonics, spelling, grammar, science, math.

How to Use this Study Guide

#1) Determine your time frame. Decide how much time to devote to each phase of the unit. Our suggestion is that you spend one week per phase - one month to cycle through the unit - which would require 12 months to complete this study. Be alert to natural calendar interruptions (like holidays or relatives coming) and plan to conclude the unit before that break. Feel free to adjust this for the needs, ages, interests of your family.

#2) There are some supplies needed. The shopping list includes:
→ Purchasing a notebook for each of your students which will be used as their **History Journal**. This will be the place to record questions, insights, personal application, short biographies of important people, or anything else that the student finds interesting. Use it every day.
→ A set of maps and a timeline for this study guide. You can either make your own or purchase the **Maps/Timeline Pack** which was made specifically to accompany this study guide.
→ A 3-ring binder to hold all of the papers generated by this study guide. Make sure the History Journal you purchase will fit into the 3-ring binder!
→ Art supplies as needed for the students' activities.

#3) Go to the library prior to the beginning of each unit to find and reserve all the materials that apply to that unit. Be thorough to order through inter-library loan all the available, related materials. Over the next few days and weeks you will be receiving all kinds of wonderful materials, so prepare a place for these treasures and introduce them to your students.

#4) Choose the items from each phase that most interest and are most appropriate for your students, and correlate them with the library resources you have discovered. Since your students are all unique, each student may choose to pursue a different aspect of the phase. This may result in different projects accomplished, different books used, or different presentations of what has been learned. This diversity will provide for your family a wonderfully broad look at each time period.

#5) Preview with the family the pertinent Bible passages which are listed in each unit. Be sure to relate all that is learned about these early civilizations to God's perspective as revealed in Scripture.

#6) Read your materials, discuss the questions, do the research, mark the timeline, draw the maps, complete your chosen hands-on activities, do the creative writing, and then, enjoy your students' final presentations!

Worldviews in the Study of History:
Our Approach to History

When Bill and I were attending a secular university, I took some anthropology courses. Anthropology is the scientific study of mankind, especially its origins, development, customs, and beliefs. At the very introduction to General Anthropology, I was alarmed and put on guard because it was announced that Christian missionaries were **always destructive** to the cultures they went to convert; that by changing the primitive peoples' belief systems and destroying their uniqueness with a western religion, the missionaries had ruined them. In sharp contrast, the anthropologists were engaged in the "scientific" study of these people groups and wouldn't think of changing anything about them (much like a "nature" photographer will take pictures of predators killing a baby elephant without doing anything to help preserve the life of the baby.)

One particular people group that we studied extensively in this class made a deep and lasting impression on me. They were the Dani of Irian Jaya (Papau New Guinea shares the same South Pacific island). The anthropologists studying the Dani had filmed them during the time that a small argument between a few escalated into a violent battle with many men killed. Throughout the film and the documents prepared on the Dani, we were "treated" to a look at a Stone Age tribe that was brutal, violent, aggressive, and dominated by a religion of evil spirits. This "scientific study" of the Dani left me with the sense of darkness and hopelessness because of the despair and depravity in this people group.

Twenty years later, we picked up the book, **Torches of Joy** by John Dekker (YWAM Publishing). Can you imagine the astonishment and delight when I discovered that this book was about a Christian missionary family that devoted themselves to the Dani people?! It described a complete, miraculous turnaround for these precious "Stone Age" people. The Dani burned their fetishes, forsook tribal warfare, and began to walk in the joy and freedom of their deliverer, Jesus Christ. The missionaries taught them basic medical knowledge, hygiene, nutrition; built fish ponds and imported fish so the Dani could increase the protein in their meager diets; helped set up trade stores which the Dani owned and operated; taught them how to read, so they could read the Bible in the newly written form of their oral language; discipled them in Biblical principles so the Dani men began to truly love their wives (rather than treating them as slaves), as well as loving their neighbors as themselves; appointed native leadership for the young church, which resulted in Dani missionaries actually going out to other tribal peoples in Irian Jaya!

The difference between these two approaches, between the "scientific study" of a Stone Age tribe by the anthropologists and the compassionate, life giving ministry of the Christian missionaries, is the difference between darkness and light; the difference between secular humanism and biblical Christianity; it reveals how godless man looks at cultures and how God looks at people. Seeing with God's heart will prevent bigotry and hate, replacing it with outreach and compassion.

As we study ancient civilizations together, please remember this illustration because it will be the difference between

- learning merely the facts and figures of a people group,

OR

- seeing fully the loving heart of God towards those people.

The first will give head knowledge of important data that may impress our audience, and make us think that we really know a lot. However, the second will give heart understanding of God's involvement in human history, so that we might be effective ministers in obedience to the Lord of all.

As we learn the details of history, of ancient civilizations, of kingdoms and empires, scientific discoveries, explorations, and more, we will begin to see God's fingerprint on the lives of people and cultures. History will become a window of adventure as we observe His faithfulness and provision for those who seek Him, His timing in raising up one nation and bringing down another, His perfect ability to work through imperfect people, and His wonderful plan to bring us to Himself, which is revealed in the Bible.

Worldviews Applied

As we begin reading books about historic people, events, empires, etc., it will become increasingly obvious that a historic fact may be interpreted to mean different things, depending on the author. Different interpretations might be evaluated as right or wrong by Christians reading the book. To determine which is right we must be aware of how the differences arise, and what they look like.

For instance, the Epic of Gilgamesh, *a legend about the Flood from the ancient civilization of Sumer, may be interpreted:*

- by one historian as evidence that the Hebrews "borrowed" their Flood story (with Noah and the ark) from an older civilization that had suffered a tremendous localized flood. He will say, "Here is the evidence that the Bible is merely a Hebrew mythology of events from a time long before they existed!" *(Think about it for a while...)*
- by another historian, the same Epic of Gilgamesh will be interpreted to be a faulty, though partly accurate, rendition of the Biblical worldwide, catastrophic Flood. He will say, "This is the evidence that there truly was a Flood which covered the entire earth! You see, every ancient culture has some form of Flood memory, though their retelling is the stuff of legends rather than the true history revealed in the Bible."

Why do such divergent opinions come from the same historic writing? The answer can be found by understanding worldviews. A "worldview" may be defined as an overarching system of belief about God, the origin of life, the purpose and meaning of life, man's relationship to God. It is such a foundational part of our being, that many people don't even know why they believe what they do.

"There is a flow to history and culture. This flow is rooted and has its wellspring in the thoughts of people. Most people catch their [world view] from their family and surrounding society the way a child catches measles. But people with more understanding realize that their presuppositions should be chosen after a careful consideration of what world view is true."
Dr. Francis Schaeffer

A tremendous book about building a Biblical worldview in your children is **Let Us Highly Resolve** by David & Shirley Quine, Cornerstone Curriculum Project. See the Resource List for ordering info.

Here is a brief summary of the prominent worldviews in the Western world (you may find these listed under different names in another source):

- Secular Humanist Worldview (2 variations)

    #1. No supernatural, nothing outside of natural forces (closed system), meaninglessness, individual is not important, ruled by an elite, no absolutes, everything is relative, evolutionary processes, history means nothing.

    #2. (The Marxist-Leninist) No supernatural, nothing outside of natural forces, meaning is found in the economic struggle toward communism, individual is not important - the State rules, no absolutes (except the eventual triumph of communism!), everything is relative, evolutionary processes, history shows the economic evolution to communism.

- Cosmic Humanist Worldview

    New Age, supernatural accepted (as long as the Judeo-Christian God is denied), meaning is found in the cosmic evolution of man rediscovering that he is god, individual is god, no absolutes (except of course that there are ABSOLUTELY no absolutes!), history points to the Age of Aquarius - the evolutionary leap into perfection.

- Biblical Worldview

    God (the God of the Bible) is the Creator; though natural processes are the norm, God is able to intervene supernaturally in history (open-system); meaning is found in restored relationship through God's redemption of man through the death and resurrection of Jesus Christ; man is a sinner in need of redemption; there are absolute truths and absolute standards that never change; history reveals God's plan and His ways of accomplishing that plan.

> *With this understanding, let us return to the dilemma concerning which historian to believe in regards to the Epic of Gilgamesh. Using the worldview descriptions above:*
> - *Which historian holds to a Biblical worldview?*
> - *Which historian holds to a secular humanist worldview?*
> - *How does that impact their interpretation of the Sumerian epic?*

It should be obvious that if a historian does not believe in the supernatural, does not believe that the Bible could have been written under the inspiration of God, does not believe that God destroyed the world (except for Noah and his family) , then they could not possibly interpret the <u>Epic of Gilgamesh</u> to be an indication of the truth of the Biblical Flood. It follows that any further interpretations made by this historian would also be suspect to readers following a Biblical worldview.

Something to Consider!

Should we only read books that are written in the Biblical Worldview?

- If our answer is **"Yes"** then we will be very limited in the number of resources available to us, though the worldview and perspective may be acceptable.

#1   Look for biblical archaeology reports.

#2   The account written by the Jewish historian, Josephus, may be acceptable.

#3   Utilize a good study Bible or handbook. It will contain good information.

#4   Read historical fiction dealing with this time period, written by Christian authors (though the number of these books is very small.)

However, this is but a small percentage of the factual, biographical, historical information accessible to us and our students.

- If our answer is **"No"** then we will read other books, using discernment, and measuring them with the following criteria.

#1   The Bible is and remains the final authority in questions of history.

For instance, during the 1700's and early 1800's, many historians scoffed at the idea that the Assyrians had been a major empire since nothing was known about them apart from the Biblical references. That all changed in the mid 1800's with the discovery of Ninevah, Khorsabad, Nimrud, and more. The Bible's historical record was vindicated.

#2   Establish guidelines and watch for key phrases to determine the author's worldview.

For example, the word "primitive man", or the phrase "man evolved over thousands and thousands of years" are warning flags to indicate the author's worldview. This does not mean the book is worthless or without value to you! Simply be aware of these warning flags - they enable you to "sift" out the chaff and leave the wheat. You can read the facts and use the pictures, but sift out the statements of interpretation or cause.

#3   We must read "critically" so that we understand the difference between the facts of history, and an author's interpretation.

People, empires, events all happened in history. We can learn much about these from various authors, as long as we recognize when an interpretation about these facts is being made.

#4   Your own sensibilities will determine when an author's bias so colors the book, that "enough is enough!"

Return the book to the library.

#5   Have your family read a number of different authors who have written about a particular time period. This will enable you to see the facts of history, then the worldviews of the authors will become more obvious.

The major facts, events and people will be the same, and the various viewpoints expressed in the several books may give you a better understanding of what really took place.

#6   Studying various aspects such as art, architecture, military strategies, local geography, artifacts, ancient writings and more, will provide a broad understanding of a particular time period.

This prepares the student to recognize an author's potential misrepresentation of the historical record.

<u>Remember!</u>

> When we read someone's work, we can:
> - appreciate it
> - enjoy it
> - understand it
>
> BUT, most importantly, we must
> - **evaluate** it!

A Note about Worldviews and Art

Throughout this study we will be examining some of the artistic endeavors of each culture represented. Some of these art works may be occasionally offensive to you, or inappropriate for younger children. So, why include them?

> * **One of the important points of this study is to understand ancient people - what they did and who they were. Ancient artwork is one of the best clues we have in learning about these people and their cultures.**

Here are some examples of the type of things you will encounter.

- Sculpture - In ancient Sumer, people believed they should always pray to their gods. However, when they had something else to do, in order to fulfill their belief, the people left statues of themselves praying to these gods!!

- Frescoes - Ancient Egyptians (especially royalty) prepared all of their lives for death and the afterlife. Archaeologists have uncovered many beautiful paintings on the inside walls of tombs which had been painted in accordance to stringent rules so as to ensure that the gods would always understand them!

- Vase Painting - The gods of the ancient Greeks were simply "bigger than life" immortals with all of the lusts, passions, cruelties and sins possible to people on earth. Perhaps worshiping these fallible gods is what led to the perspective that the human body, unclothed, was the paramount expression of beauty. Whatever the reason, Greek athletes usually competed in the nude, and much of the existing art of ancient Greece deals with nudes. (I did "toss" from my recommended reading list the books on ancient Greece that were too graphic! You may, however, still occasionally find some things you don't like. Skip it and keep going.)

- Clothing - On the isle of Crete, a magnificent palace was uncovered by archaeologists. Within this Minoan palace, marvelous mosaics and frescoes were found. One of the scientists from France saw the portraits of ancient Minoan women and remarked that they looked as if they were recently returned from Paris! Inexplicably, the women's dresses left part of the body uncovered so they seem quite immodest to our culture. No one has discovered the reason for this, but the extraordinary fashionableness of the Minoan women does express something unique about this culture.

So Many Books, So Little Time! - Using the Library

Unless we have the opportunity to:
- actually go to the Middle East,
- visit all the museums,
- join in the archaeological digs,
- accompany biblical archaeologists in their searches,
- interview the original discoverers of ancient civilizations,

we will not really comprehend the cultures of antiquity.
That is, UNLESS we read books!!

Books will unlock the doors to learning:

- *meet Austen Layard, a British adventurer who discovered the forgotten city of Ninevah, unknown until 1854 except in the biblical references;*
- *share the discovery by Sir Arthur Evans of an unknown culture on the island of Crete, the Minoans;*
- *learn how Leonard Wooley, the man who excavated Ur, employed on the dig one who would later be known as Lawrence of Arabia;*
- *see Howard Carter as he opens the only untouched tomb of a Pharaoh ever discovered - the unimaginable splendor of King Tut;*
- *discover how the seven wonders of the ancient world were built, and how long they existed;*
- *learn how the Bible as history has been verified time after time, even to the most minute details.*

Where do we learn all of these wonderful, fascinating, intriguing details? In books written by the archaeologists, books about the archaeologists, books describing the civilizations uncovered by the archaeologists, books telling how to recreate what the archaeologists found... books, books, and more books! There are books about art, architecture, wars, city planning, construction techniques, "mysteries" of ancient civilizations and more. There are picture books, children's books, fictional books, boring books, fascinating books, books to be shared and books to be discarded.

Does this mean we need to take out a second mortgage to purchase all of these books?! NO! It means we need to become well acquainted with our library, our librarians, the inter-library loan system, the university libraries, the state libraries, school libraries, and church libraries, and your friends' and neighbors' libraries. The library system is a wonderful resource - learn how to use it!

Here are some suggestions on how to get the most out of your library:

#1　Enlist the help of the librarians - tell them what you're doing and what you're looking for - they probably will be delighted to help you!

#2　Search the computer/card catalog for subject areas as well as titles and authors (i.e. Ancient Rome, children's fiction).

#3　Check out several books on the same subject - this gives a broader understanding as well as giving more choices of which ones look interesting to your students.

#4　Keep a record of the books, return them promptly in excellent condition!

Learning Styles

This study guide has been designed to incorporate the four learning styles into each unit. For the parent/teacher this is not a constant cause for decision making and possibly confusing choices, but an assurance of thoroughness on the author's part - there will be material to attract each of your students, and to provide a multi-faceted approach to understanding history.

A brief explanation of these four learning styles follows (for more information, please read Diana Waring's **Beyond Survival: A Guide to Abundant Life Homeschooling**, Cynthia Tobias' book **The Way They Learn**, or Alta Vista's **Learning Styles and Tools**.) What follows is a sketch of each of the learning styles. Perhaps you will recognize your students among these descriptions.

The Feeler

This is the "people person" learning style. A Feeler wants to know the people perspective, i.e. how this subject affects people, how does this impact our lives now, who were the people of history as opposed to the events or the things? This learner needs to be in good relationship with the people around him - his teacher, siblings, friends, etc. They love to be with other people in one-on-one conversations and in group activities, especially when they are part of a "team effort".

The Thinker

"Give me the facts, ma'am, just the facts." The Thinker has a black & white approach to knowledge, wanting authoritative input, not just someone's opinions. This learner truly enjoys using textbooks, encyclopedias, charts, diagrams. There is a need to know exactly what is expected, when it is expected, what, exactly, are the requirements of an assignment, project, etc. They are organized and expect organization.

The Sensor

The "hands-on", get-it-done-now person! The Sensor is the one who can make projects happen - taking them beyond the "blueprint" stage and into production. This learner does NOT enjoy sitting for long periods of time, looking through books for information (which is the Thinker's cup of tea!), or cuddling up on the couch to discuss things for hours on end (which appeals to the Feeler!). Instead, the Sensor prefers to be involved with things that can be efficiently accomplished, and that require more physical than mental work.

The Intuitor

"Wait! I have an idea!" The Intuitor is the one brimming over with ideas about how this might have happened, or about how your family might put on a play for the whole city portraying an historic event, or about what it must have been like to live in ancient times, and on and on. This learner is very good at coming up with suggestions, but is much less interested in seeing things through to completion. The Intuitor needs a lot of flexibility in schedule, and a "safe haven" for suggesting and trying out ideas. (It's not helpful to squash ALL of their ideas, no matter how bizarre!!!)

Learning Modalities

There is often confusion about the differences between the four learning styles and the terms visual, auditory and kinesthetic. To clarify what is meant by "learning modalities" (i.e. visual, auditory, kinesthetic), consider this analogy. A friend from the other side of the country wants to come to your house for a visit. They may choose to fly, to take the train, or to come by bus - whichever they prefer. In the same way, each of us has a preferred method of transporting information to our brains. Some grasp new material best by reading it (visual), others by hearing someone talk (auditory), still others by manipulating it (kinesthetic).

Any of these modalities can be found in each of the four learning styles. For instance, your son may be a Thinker who receives information best by hearing it, while your daughter may be a Thinker who must read the instructions in order to remember them. You may be a Sensor who needs to simply pull all the nuts and bolts out of the bag to assemble the kit (forget reading the instructions!) Perhaps your spouse is an Intuitor who can figure out how to create a new brick design after simply seeing samples in a book, while your Intuitor neighbor could hear a description of a new recipe for cherry pie and then springboard off into a new recipe for cherry coffeecake.

Please remember, these are not labels intended to put a person into a "box." Rather, they are tools that help us understand and appreciate one another. Particularly, if you find that a student is not grasping the material, or is in conflict with you about an assignment, be sure to consider these learning styles and learning modalities to see if perhaps you could use a different approach in your presentation.

Cycle Approach Used in Each Unit

With these four learning styles in mind, the cycle approach used in this study guide will begin with a phase to introduce the people involved, which the Feeler will love. Then we will proceed to the "hard facts" phase, which excites the Thinker. The next phase will be right up the Sensor's alley with lots of hands-on projects, followed by the open-ended "possibilities" phase which will make the Intuitor soar. All students, regardless of their learning style, will benefit from this four-phase cycle approach because it reinforces the new material over and over again. Also, because each of us have a combination of learning styles, learning modalities, as well as giftings, talents and interests, the cycle approach will provide a well-rounded blend of study activities for each of your unique students.

Here are some of the types of projects contained in our cycle approach:

Phase #1: *Grab 'Em!* (the Feeler)

History:

- **What in the World's Going on Here?** tapes
- The names of the People, Places, Events
- Preview Presentation - Video, Audio, Read aloud, Explain
- Interview craftsmen, experts, etc.
- "If you were there" - intro to the impact of the location and terrain on people and cultures
- Discussing the impact of a ruler on conquered people
- Learning about family issues
- Talking about what it would be like to be a slave; a peasant; a soldier, an emperor

English:

- Reading Biographies, Historical Fiction
- Answer the question "who-how?" in written or verbal form
- Snapshot bio (most important aspects of a person's life) written in the history journal or in a separate notebook
- Journal - regular entry to track what is being learned

Art:

- Draw people in history to complement journal
- Color in TimeCharts

Phase #2: *Teach 'Em!* (the Thinker)

History:

- Identify and follow strands - warfare, technology, apparel, architecture, people groups, agriculture, transportation, etc.
- Seminar outline from **What in the World's Going on Here?**
- Build a timeline
- Vocabulary list
- Research and report
- Compile additional information for personalized unit studies
- "When?" in relation to other events, other civilizations
- Charting out each empire's key leaders, cities, wars, etc.

English:

- Reading factual accounts of history
- Written or verbal or video report
- Answer the "why?", "what?", "how?"
- Researching in library - Periodicals, Non-Fiction History section
- Summarizing, compiling
- Write foreign embassies, government departments

Computer:

- On line - check out information available on the Internet (Caution: parental supervision)
- CD-ROM discs about history

Phase #3: *Apply 'Em!* (the Sensor)

Geography:

- Maps to fill in
- Topographical maps - to study
- Papier Maché maps - to make
- Learn climate, terrain

Arts and Crafts:

- Models
- Pottery... Clay sculpting
- Collage
- Hieroglyphics, Cuneiform, Printing, Paper Making
- Costuming
- Making props for productions
    - Papier Maché - puppet heads, masks, mosaics, buildings
    - Painting
    - Observation - Paintings, sculptures, artwork
    - Cooking
    - Feasts of Israel: Tabernacles, Passover, Purim, Hanukkah, Sabbath
- Video Productions - Computer Art
- Copper tooling
- Drawing, coloring
- Building replicas of bridges, bricks, walled cities, and more

Music:

- Listening
- Creating instruments
- The Five Elements of music
- Singing
- Creating your own!

Science and Math:

- Experimentation & Discovery

Phase #4: *Release 'Em!* (the Intuitor)

Creative Writing:

- Short story
- Fictional account - "The World's Oldest Novel"... or "Bob, the Coppersmith, builds idols for Cain"
- Illustrate a children's book
- Poetry
- Rhymes
- Puns, jokes
- Retell using modern names, terms
- Keep a history journal with entries about the new thoughts, questions, and answers the study is provoking
- Write a story, "A day in the life of..."

Art:

- Cartoons
- Illustrations

Drama:

- Role-playing
- Puppet shows
- Musical - suggested Bible scene with hymns, worship choruses
- Plays

Extrapolate:

- "How did...?" questions
- "What if...?" questions
- Build own version of **Timetables of History**
- Plan a presentation using drama, music, art, puppetry - which explains what has been learned in the unit
- Teach the younger students about some aspect of living in an ancient culture using a creative approach to capture their attention

Family Style Studies

We have always found that studying history together as a family makes it fascinating! Since we all have such different interests, studying as a family allows many more topic discussions to come up, many more rabbit trails to be followed, and many varying opinions about "why this happened" to be expressed. There is a "synergy" - (synergy = the whole is greater than the sum of the parts) - that occurs when the whole family researches different aspects of a civilization and then shares them with each other!

NOTE: Preschoolers are obviously not up to the "research" mode yet, but they can certainly be involved with skits, building duplo forts, throwing a frisbee (the descendant of the Greek discus!), tasting the "authentic" recipes, etc.

Here are some suggestions about how to make history a "family time!":

#1 Keep a common thread running in the family. One of the best ways we have found is to read aloud the most interesting book that will appeal to everyone.
(We have found several fascinating books covering a tremendous variety of topics. Also, the Bible is ALWAYS a good suggestion when reading about ancient times. Make sure to read it dramatically!)

#2 Ask open ended questions and assignments so each can answer in their own way...
→ Of all the things we've learned about this culture, what aspect has been most interesting (i.e. art, writing, weaponry, etc.) to you? OK, do a project on that!
→ Research the everyday life in this ancient culture of a farmer, a soldier, a mother, a daughter, a ruler - whatever you would have wanted to be. Then tell us about it.
→ What would YOU have done if God had told you to go to Ninevah during the time of Jonah?

#3 Get lots of books from the library and from other resources that deal with a variety of topics pertinent to the time period. Do not assign which books the children must read, rather allow them to choose what look's interesting to them - and then let them tell the others what they learned from that book.
(For instance, my son Michael picked up a book about Hannibal crossing the Alps with elephants. He thought it was so interesting that he told me I needed to read it too - which I promptly did!)

#4 Provide lots of opportunities to share with each other about what is being learned. This is not a "test" , but an "I can't wait to tell you about this!" atmosphere. Dinner time, car rides across town, last half hour before bed, walks to the park are all great times for sharing the fascinating "stuff" you're learning.

A Multi-Discipline, Multi-Sensory Approach

History is the story of everything that has ever happened from the moment of Creation until the present. This includes discoveries of new continents, inventions of high tech computers, the lifestyles of emperors and slaves, every day usage of upper level mathematics, art masterpieces, musical parodies and more. Because of this, it is very natural to incorporate other subjects into your history study.

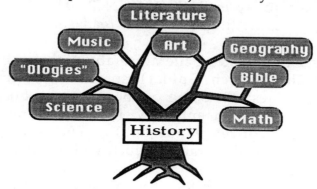

Science -

Science fits into history as we learn about the discoveries, the inventions, and the explorations which occurred in a time period. The student can recreate these scientific moments through experiments which will both help him to understand history and recognize the importance of science.

Geography -

Learning the geography of a location is essential if we are going to truly understand history. When you are considering trade or commerce or conquest, the hindrance of a desert or mountain range will become as obvious as the benefit of temperate climate and coastal cities. By mapping the local geography of an ancient culture and contrasting it to the location of modern cities and countries, the student will have a firm understanding of the where's and the why's of history.

Art -

Art is found both in everyday objects, such as pottery, as well as incredible masterpieces, such as frescoes. People of almost every culture have an art expression of some kind, and examining this will help the student to understand the people of a culture at a much deeper level. Jewelry, sculpture, painting, pottery, mosaics, clothing (fabrics, colors, designs) and more are all things we're going to be looking at in this study. From this list will come possible projects for the student to pursue in the exploration of this subject in ancient history.

Math -

Math is a foundational subject, and has always been so. When we look at ancient cultures and see buildings, temples, etc., we are seeing math in action (all the way from adding the workers' wages to engineering the pyramids!) This study will look at both the mathematicians of antiquity and their discoveries.

Literature -

In studying ancient civilizations, we will discover the history of writing (cuneiform, hieroglyphics, and more) as well as the content of what ancient civilizations wrote about! Some archaeological digs have uncovered vast libraries of clay bricks inscribed with cuneiform. These libraries include literature, laws, lists, etc. Other digs have uncovered only bookkeeping records (this much for a bushel of wheat, etc.). The story of how these ancient writings were finally translated so we could understand them today is FASCINATING! The student in this study will learn about the history of writing, and, also, read some of the translated texts of antiquity.

We will also spend time reading literature **about** these civilizations. Some will be modern (such as **The Golden Goblet**), some will be hundreds of years old (Shakespeare's "Julius Caesar"). Some of the literature books will be simplified translations of books written in antiquity, like **The Exploits of Xenophon** by Xenophon, edited by Geoffrey Household. The student will have ample opportunity to read wonderful literature which will expand their understanding of history.

Writing will also be utilized as the student progresses in the study of history. This study guide will provide opportunities for creative writing, report writing, history journal, newspaper-style reporting, letters to Grandma, business letters (to embassies, travel agencies, airlines, etc), drama sketches, poetry, and more.

Music -

Musical instruments have been found in the tombs of earliest civilization. Though not much is known about the style of music played, this study guide will indicate what has been learned about music in antiquity. The family can certainly "make their own" music when performing a dramatic presentation, or fashion musical instruments and play them (even if it does sound like a hootenanny.) Music makes the study of history come to life!

All those "Ologies" -

This study guide will also introduce students to subject areas such as archaeology, anthropology, paleontology, and more, though they might not always be named as such. Instead, we will focus on learning everything we can about ancient cultures which will help us to understand them better. Such things as family customs, burial rites, weapons and warfare, slavery, trade routes, empire-building, and occupations will enhance a student's knowledge of history.

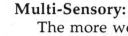

Multi-Sensory:
The more we can use the five senses in our study of history, the more exciting and memorable it will be.
Try these:
- Smell it! (Bake, craft, sniff a barn, etc.)
- Taste it! (Cook it - sweet? salty? bitter? sour?)
- Touch it! (Woods, metals, bricks, skins, pots, etc.)
- See it! (Pictures, books, videos, field trips, etc.)
- Hear it! (Read outloud, tapes, music, etc.)

Record Keeping & Evaluations

There are many different ways to track your student's work and progress. High school students will need a more thorough record kept than elementary students, and different teachers prefer different methods of keeping track of what's been accomplished. For a thorough description of record keeping, please check your state's requirements (available through homeschool support groups), and refer to such resources as Gayle Graham's **How to Homeschool**, Diana McAllister's **Homeschooling the Highschooler**, Diana Waring's **Beyond Survival: A Guide to Abundant Life Homeschooling**, and other books.

Some possibilities for tracking the work are:

- Keep a simple log of books read, projects done, topics covered (can be done by student or teacher)

- Make a portfolio of major projects completed

- Record the hours spent, subject studied

- Plan objectives with student, determine whether objectives were met (contract agreement)

- There are twelve units in this study and records can be kept accordingly:
    - each unit can be recorded separately (i.e. Greece, Rome...)
    - the entire study guide can be treated as one course (Ancient Civ.)

Some possibilities for evaluating the work are:

- Narration - allow your students to tell in their own words about what has been read (a wonderful way to discover whether they fully understand the important points of a book)

- Discussion - ask open-ended questions to permit a free flowing conversation about what is being learned. (For instance, "What would you have thought about King Cyrus of Persia conquering Babylon if you had been a Jew in captivity? A Babylonian peasant? A Persian soldier?")

- Presentation - give opportunity for your students to share what they have learned in a more formal setting. (Perhaps your students will want to stage a Passover feast after studying Egypt and the Exodus, and will explain to your guests the significance of this feast)

- Written reports - fictional stories, poetry, dramas, essay questions, research reports, and more are all possible means of determining your student's mastery of the subject

Bloom's Taxonomy

For those who are interested, Bloom's Taxonomy is a tool to help teachers establish their educational objectives. Highly regarded and widely used among educators, it is used to assure that a course of study challenges the thought processes of each student from the youngest to the most developed.

In our study guide, we have followed the wisdom of using Bloom's Taxonomy in the development of our lesson suggestions. (**Important Note:** You DON'T need to understand Bloom's Taxonomy in order to benefit from the use of it in this study guide!)

Incorporated throughout **Ancient Civilizations and the Bible: A "Digging Deeper" Study Guide** are questions, activities, and assignments that cover the range of the six categories described in **Bloom's Taxonomy**:

- Knowledge: Remembering, drilling, listing, repeating

- Comprehension: Understanding, identifying, reviewing, explaining, reporting

- Application: Solving, using, interpreting, demonstrating, illustrating

- Analysis: Analyzing, experimenting, debating, comparing, questioning

- Synthesis: Creating, formulating, designing, arranging

- Evaluation: Judging, evaluating, appraising, establishing criteria

Resource List

Most of the books listed in this study guide are available from the library or inter-library loan. However, the creationist books, the Christian titles and a few of the other wonderful resources listed will have to be purchased from homeschool providers, Christian bookstores, etc. The following is a list of some of the homeschool providers we know carry these materials. Call for their catalogs. *There are many other booksellers out there who may also be able to help you.*

Farm Country General Store
1-800-551-3276

Great Christian Books
1-800-775-5422

Sing & Learn
1-972-278-1973

Lifetime Books and Gifts
1-800-377-0390

The Book Peddler
1-216-323-9494

Home Learning Center
1-406-257-5440

Family Christian Academy
1-615-860-3000

Bend Cornerstone Books
1-541-389-0772

Rainbow Resources
1-309-937-3385

Children's Books
1-800-344-3198

Focus on the Family
1-800-232-6459 - Videos

Diana Waring - History Alive!
1-605-642-7583

YWAM Publishing
1-800-922-2143

ZCI Publishing (CD Roms)
1-214-746-5510

Builder Books
1-509-826-6021

Valor Resources
1-800-40 VALOR (pin #85)
(**Make it Work!** books)

Cobblestone Soap
(215) 249-3647
(Great soap-making kits!)

Five in a Row
1-816-331-5769
(For younger ones - it's great!)

Cornerstone Curriculum Project
1-214-235-5149

Geography Matters
1-800-426-4650

Ferg 'N Us
1-610-282-0401

Unit One

The Creation

Unit Objectives:

- to gain a biblical foundation for the beginnings of history; to be familiar with the order of events of Creation and early Genesis;

- to appreciate the incredible beauty, order and intricacy of God's creation;

- to recognize in world history the impact of the Fall of man;

- to understand the tenets of creationism vs. evolution; be able to compare/contrast them;

- to investigate the implications of the historical fact that God created man as an intelligent, capable creature.

Meet the People

- **The Holy Bible**
  Genesis 1- 4, Job 38:4 - 41:34, Psalm 8:3-9, Psalm 19:1-6, Psalm 65:5-13, Psalm 89: 11-14, Psalm 95:1-7, Psalm 100, Psalm 104, Psalm 136:1-9, Psalm 148, Isaiah 40:12-31, Jeremiah 32:17, Matthew 19:4-6, John 1:1-5, Romans 1:20, Colossians 1:15-17, Hebrews 1:10, 11:3

- **The Bible Time Nursery Rhyme Book** by Emily Hunter
  For the little ones in your family, this is the sweetest, most delightful book that we know about the events of the Bible.   **Preschool and up.**

- **Unlocking the Mysteries of Creation** by Dennis Peterson
  This is an eye-opening book about Creation! Divided into three sections, it deals with evidences for a young earth, the questions about fossils and dinosaurs, and fascinating discoveries showing the astonishing accomplishments of early man (early civilizations).   **Great for the family!**

- **Adam & His Kin** by Ruth Beechick
  A speculative, but fascinating look at what life may have been like during the first several chapters of Genesis.   **Great read aloud!**

- **The Great Dinosaur Mystery and the Bible** by Paul S. Taylor
  Children often want to know, "But, Mommy! What about the dinosaurs?" when we talk about Creation. This is a great picture book to introduce the answers on a child's level (though I learned a lot too!)   **Elementary and up.**

- **Understanding The Times** (abridged edition) by David Noebel
  This book (especially Ch. 15 through 18) will greatly help to clarify the worldview positions of evolutionists and creationists. We think it is absolutely critical to understand the issue of worldview, and of its impact on every branch of learning. Dr. Noebel has written an excellent resource.   **High School and up.**

- **Darwin on Trial** by Phillip E. Johnson
  "The controversial book that rocked the scientific establishment! Why? It shows that the theory of evolution is based not on fact but on faith - faith in philosophical naturalism." This fascinating book was written by a professor of law, and is laid out so simply that the non-scientist can follow the arguments. It is very helpful for understanding the fallacies in the evolutionist argument.
  High School and up.

Talk Together

- Listen to What in the World's Going on Here?, Tape One. What was the most interesting aspect to you of the events in Creation which were mentioned? Why? What questions do you have about this time period that you would like to learn more about?

    History Journal: Write those questions down, and as you study more material, write the answers to your questions. Write short bios of the interesting people. Illustrate the bios.

- Read the first two chapters of Genesis. What did God create? What groups are named and what specific things are named? From what did God create? From what did He form Adam? ... Eve? What was necessary in order for Adam to become a living soul?

- Look in a Bible handbook or commentary to discover more information. Where do scholars believe the Garden of Eden was located? Can we know for certain? Why or why not?

- Would you have enjoyed being the one to name the animals? How many names would you have needed to find? Which of Adam's names are in use still?

- Why did Adam and Eve choose to disobey God and eat the forbidden fruit? What reason is given in the Bible? What are some of the results of their choice? How did that impact every person born after them? (**Hint:** Look in the Bible for these terms: creation, rest, first Adam / second Adam, redemption, grace.) What did God do to restore us to relationship with Him?

    History Journal: consider these questions and how they impact you personally. What is your own personal experience with these issues - do you have forgiveness through the second Adam? History really does affect us, from even the very beginning of time!

- Why do you think God gave us the description of pre-flood technology? How does a biblical worldview in its picture of earliest human history and technology compare to an evolutionary worldview?

- One of Cain's descendants was Tubal-Cain, who was an instructor of every craftsman in bronze and iron. (Genesis 4:22) This man demonstrates that pre-Flood man had obtained a much higher level of technology than we have been led to believe. What other indications are there of pre-flood technology and intelligence? (**Hint:** Music is considered to be a significant advancement in technology, and most evolutionists believe that it is a later development of mankind.)

- What are some of the implications of an intelligent "early man?" (**Hint:** If Thomas Edison had lived in pre-flood times, with a life span similar to what is described in Genesis, what might he have invented?)

- Who are the people of this pre-flood section? What are their actions? Are they promoting godliness or rebellion? Are they "prehistoric"? Are these people similar to us, or different from us? In what ways?

Teaching Time!

Seminar Outline

◇ I. Creation - Stone-Age Man versus Genesis 4:22
◇   *"And as for Zillah, she also bore Tubal-Cain, an instructor of every c craftsman in bronze and iron."*
◇   A) Were there really 35,000 years of Stone-Age Man?
◇   B) Tubal-Cain was 8th generation from Adam
◇   C) Technology of Metallurgy?
◇   1) Bronze - alloy of copper and tin
◇   2) Iron - one of the most difficult to reduce from its' ore
◇   D) Jubal, the first musician
◇   1) Complexity of music
◇   2) Technological advancement

Timeline

No one knows exactly when Adam and Eve were created, except God! There have been some who, using the genealogies in the Old Testament, have calculated that man was created about 4,500 B.C. Others believe that the genealogies do not necessarily contain every generation born, so they think that man could have been created as early as 10,000 B.C. Still others consider that the archaeological evidence and carbon dating indicate that earliest man appeared about 35,000 B.C. Read and compare anthropologists accounts from both the creationist and evolutionist view.

→   On your timeline mark the creation of man at the beginning of the chart. My suggestion would be to date it at approximately 5,000 B.C. so that you don't have huge empty spaces in between Creation and the next events.

Research & Reporting:

- Find one of the books listed on the first page of this unit, along with other creation science/intelligent design books for basic information on Creation and evolution. Outline their important points.

2-J • Read Genesis and the New Testament scriptures about Creation. Do the writers of the New Testament, as well as the words of Jesus, indicate they believed the Bible account of Creation was literal history? Write a defense for your position.

1-J • Do a research paper, with pictures, on the amazing intricacies of the eye, the brain, the heart, or any other part of the human body. Include the function of the organ, and its interrelation with other organs.

3-J • Find out how scientists explain the complexity of the eye, heart, etc. in light of their belief in a mindless evolutionary process. Compare/contrast this with the scriptural account of Creation.

3-A • Research the science of metallurgy. What is required to manufacture bronze? Iron? Explain how this demonstrates technological advancement. (**Extra Credit!** Research what it would take for your family to make bronze. Give an inventory of the necessary equipment and facilities, the cost involved, and the value of the product. Is it feasible?)

- Investigate what is necessary to create and play musical instruments. If possible, interview someone who makes or repairs instruments. Ask about the technology involved and the difficulties involved in this art. Ask at your music store for a video about instrument manufacturing.

2-A • Research the term "genealogy." Collect the names and statistics of your family's ancestry, either through interviewing members of your family or researching through the library, Internet, other organizations. (Save this information for the Family Tree Project in Cycle Three.)

1-A • Make a chart listing the order of events during the Creation week.

- What was the short term result of the Fall? What was the long term result?

Vocabulary

prehistoric	technology	banish	light
antediluvian	metallurgy	repentance	day
evolution	genealogy	ancestor	night
creation	redemption	deceive	moon
origins	Fall of Man	Sabbath	sun
worldview	rebellion	earth	
naturalism	science	religion	

Hands On!

Maps and Mapping

- Because the Garden of Eden was sealed off from man's presence after Adam and Eve sinned, and since the Flood thoroughly altered the geography of the Earth, it is impossible to pinpoint today exactly where the events of Genesis 1-7 occurred. However, archaeologists believe the "cradle of civilization", or the place of earliest man, is located in the Fertile Crescent between the Tigris and Euphrates.

- Using an atlas, encyclopedia or other resource, locate the Tigris and Euphrates rivers on a map.

- On a clean worksheet map, draw the Tigris and Euphrates rivers, label the location of the Fertile Crescent. Mark the location of mountains, deserts, and current cities and countries. (We will study this area again in later chapters.)

- Give a description, either verbally or with your art tools, of the appearance of Eden.

Arts in Action

- Learning to work with copper is an interesting means of understanding what early craftsmen dealt with. Locate a hobby shop and browse through their copper crafts. Be sure to ask questions about working with this substance, trying to learn all you can. Then, when you are ready, try your hand at creating a copper "work of art." (**Hint:** If you have Visual Manna's **Teaching History Through Art**, you will have a piece of copper foil and some suggestions of how to create art with it!)

- If your family or friends are involved in any form of metal-working, be sure to ask them questions. It may be that you'll learn all about how to smelt metals (*Smelt? Sounds sort of fishy to me...*), how bronze is produced, etc.

• To learn more about metallurgy, visit your town's blacksmith shop, machine shop, or foundry.

• Follow the instructions in a science manual for experiments with molten lead.

• Visit a jewelry manufacturer to learn about their use of metals and precious stones. Try making some metal jewelry.

• Read Edith Schaeffer's book, Hidden Art. It is based upon the concept that we reflect our Creator when we create. There are many practical ideas for possible projects. Choose what appeals to you and make it! Perhaps there will be several projects within one family, and perhaps you will inspire others to be more creative. Possible areas to consider are gardening, floral arranging, cooking, clothes design, making furniture, and many more. (**Hint:** Find a book or an expert who call help you get started in your creative endeavors.)

• Make a Family Tree: On poster board, draw a large tree with branches. At the roots, label the names of the children in your family. On the first two branches, write your mother's name and your father's name. From those branches, keep adding branches as far back as you can go.

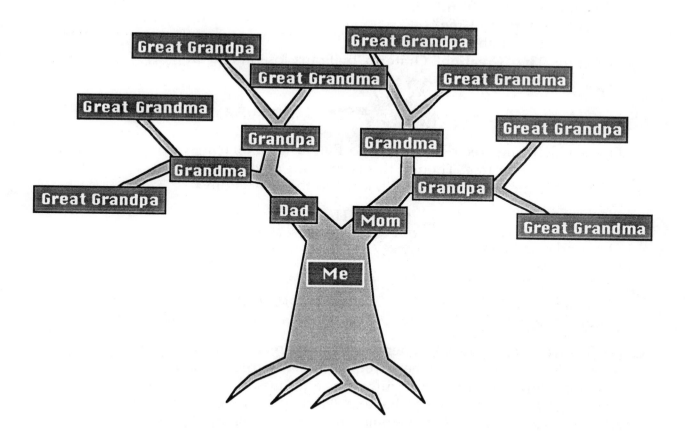

Art Appreciation

- If possible, find a picture of:
  The Sistine Chapel – Creation by Michelangelo

Does his painting reflect what the Bible describes?
How does the painting differ from your own impression of this historic event?
After observing the painting, try to draw or paint these same scenes:
- 1) imitating Michelangelo (trace, follow colors, etc.)
  (**Think about this:** Michelangelo painted the Sistine Chapel while lying on his back on scaffolding for several years! For a captivating look at his experience, watch the video, **"The Agony and the Ecstasy"**.)
- 2) creating your own picture of Creation

 Music

- **Sing hymns together:** "All Things Bright and Beautiful"
  "How Great Thou Art"
  "All Creatures of our God and King"
  "Great is Thy Faithfulness"
  "O Worship the King"
  "I Sing the Mighty Power of God"
- **Listen to: The "Creation" Oratorio** by Franz Joseph Haydn

 Cooking

From which fruit tree did Adam and Eve fashion their first clothing? That's right! It was the fig tree. Though this recipe did not come down from antediluvian times, it DOES include a fruit well known to the first family.

Fig Hermits

1/2 pound dried figs	2 3/4 cup unbleached flour
1/2 cup butter	3 tsp baking powder
3/4 cup sugar	1/2 tsp salt
2 eggs, unbeaten	2 tbsp apple juice
1/2 cup honey	1/2 cup walnuts (chopped)

Cover figs with cold water, simmer 10 min. Drain and chop. Cream butter & sugar together, add eggs and honey, beat well. Mix dry ingredients together and add to butter/sugar mixture; stir in fruit juice, figs and nuts. Drop by teaspoonfuls 2 inches apart on a greased cookie sheet. Bake in 375 degree preheated oven, 6-8 minutes (or until done). Cool slightly before removing from cookie sheet. About 4 dozen.

Idea Time!

Creative Writing

- You be the journalist, and write an article for the "First Word Times" called, "A Day in the Life of Seth."
- Compose and perform a song about Adam and Eve called, "It's Cool to be Perfect!"
- Try your hand at writing puns. Like this:

"Hey Mom, you know what you call a fly that has no wings?"
"No, son, what do you call a fly that has no wings?"

"A walk!"

- Genesis tells us that God gave Adam the job of naming all of the animals. That should give us a good indication of just how intelligent Adam was! Can you imagine naming thousands and thousands of birds, reptiles, mammals, amphibians, and... BUGS? Not to mention dinosaurs!
  - Choose five from each category above, and give them new names. Search for solid, interesting names which reflect the characteristics of the animal.
  - If that's not enough challenge, name twenty of each!
  - You could listen to Bob Dylan's song, "Man gave names to all the animals..."

Drama

- Do a humorous skit about Adam and Eve being introduced by God.
- Produce a puppet show for young children which helps them understand what life was like before the Flood.
- Act out the scene of Adam naming the animals. Let the other family members play the part of the animals. Use your imagination to create props, sets and costumes.
- Reenact the Fall of Man. Finish your presentation with the prophecies of the Redeemer.

The Big Picture

- Do a final presentation of what you've learned about God's glory in the Creation, and His mercy in providing a way of redemption.

Unit Two

Noah and the Flood

Unit Objectives:

- to learn the historical nature of the Flood, and the scientific evidences for it;

- to know the cause of God's judgment;

- to understand the role played by Noah and family in preserving mankind and repopulating the earth;

- to know the location and geology of the mountains of Ararat, and to learn about the search for the Ark;

- to find the geographical location of the descendants of Noah;

- to know the time frame for earliest civilization and the theoretical factors that account for that timing;

- to know the effect of floods, and of Noah's Flood in particular.

Meet the People

- **The Holy Bible**
  Read Genesis 5 - 10, Matthew 24:37-39, Hebrews 11:4-7, 1 Peter 3:20, 2 Peter 2:5

- **Noah's Ark** by Poortvliet
  This is an oversize beautiful book of paintings and sketches about Noah's Ark. It is quite expensive, so check to see if your library can get it.
  Great for the family!

- **The Genesis Flood** by Whitcomb and Morris
  This is an excellent resource for understanding the scientific evidences for the biblical Flood, as well as the inadequacies of evolution to explain what is seen in the geologic, archaeological, and fossil record. **High School and up.**

- **Dry Bones and Other Fossils** by Dr. Gary Parker
  Written in an engaging style for children, this is a captivating, information-filled book that will give a basic understanding of the Flood, and its impact on the earth.
  Great for the family!

- **History of the World** by Josephus Edited by Paul Maier
  Josephus was a Jewish historian who survived the destruction of Jerusalem in 70 A.D. He was taken to Rome and befriended by Emperor Titus, who asked Josephus to write an account of the history of the Jews. An original source document and one of the few histories written in antiquity, this book is a veritable gold mine of information. **High School and up.**

- **Noah, Voyage to a New Earth** by Lucas
  Out-of-print, fictionalized account of a high-tech society that is destroyed by the Flood. Not everyone likes historical fiction, but for those who do, this book is a thought-provoking look at the level of technology acquired by pre-Flood civilization. **Junior High and up.**

- **After the Flood** by Bill Cooper
  This is one of the MOST amazing books concerning the truth of the Scriptures that I have ever read! Mr. Cooper spent more than twenty years examing the accuracy of the Table of Nations in Genesis 10, and found the descendants of Ham, Shem and Japeth throughout the pagan king lists - which are the best chroniclers of families and chronologies in the ancient world. Ruth Beechick believes this is one of the watershed books of our time. Highly Recommended!
  High School and up.

Talk Together

- Listen to What in the World's Going on Here?, Tape One. What was the most interesting aspect to you of the Noah and the Flood which were mentioned? Why? What questions do you have about this time period that you would like to learn more about?

  History Journal: Write those questions down, and as you study more material, write the answers to your questions. Write short bios of the interesting people. Illustrate the bios.

- Noah, his wife, their three sons and wives were the eight people who survived the devastation of the Flood. How should that impact our attitude about other races, cultures, people groups?

- Talk about the things Noah did, according to Genesis:
    - → He built an ark, or boat, before it ever rained. How far from the water do you think Noah might have lived?
    - → He labored for many years on an object that made no sense to the people of his day, since they had never seen it rain. Do you think he would have been ridiculed? Why or why not? Describe the scoffing and hostility Noah and his family had to endure as they explained what they were building, and why. (Read Hebrews 11:7)
    - → He was a preacher of righteousness in a time when no one wanted to listen. How difficult or even dangerous do you think that might have been?
    - → He had to figure out how much food for people and animals was needed on the ark, acquire it and store it. How do you think he was able to find out what kind of food the animals needed? How was he able to calculate the amount, and how much would it have cost?
    - → He had to convince his family to get on the ark with him - do you think it was an easy thing to do? (Read about Lot getting his family out of Sodom and Gomorrah!)
    - → He had to learn how to live after the Flood with a different type of climate, a different type of soil and terrain. Genesis tells us that he planted a vineyard. Where do you suppose he got the grape vines? How did he learn about post-flood agriculture? Where did he get the tools?

- Why do you think pre-Flood man ignored the lessons from Adam and Eve's experience? Why did they all choose to turn away from their Creator, except for Noah and his family? What can we learn from this time in human history?

- Reading through the Old Testament, and studying the Church throughout history shows us the tendency for later generations to forget God and His wonderful works. Is there an antidote to this forgetfulness? What do you think? (Read Deuteronomy 6 to find some helpful suggestions.)

Teaching Time!

noah 10th gen from Adam

Seminar Outline

- ◇ II. Noah and the Flood
- ◇ A) What is the date for the rise of civilizations in modern history books?
- ◇ B) How old was Noah when the flood came?
- ◇ C) According to scripture, how old was his grandfather, Methuselah? *960*
- ◇ D) Noah's sons
- ◇ 1) Ham
- ◇ a) Ham's son, Canaan, cursed by Noah (Ge 9:25)
- b) Ham's descendants: Canaanites, Philistines, Amorites, Egyptians, Libyans, Ethiopians
- ◇ 1) Nimrod, Ham's grandson, mighty leader — *hunter*
- ◇ 2) Builder of cities: Babel, Calah or Nimrud, Ninevah
- ◇ c) Settled in the lower Middle East, Africa *beginning of kingdom* *asyria* *ur*
- ◇ 2) Shem
- ◇ a) Blessed by Noah (Ge 9:26)
- ◇ b) Shem's descendants: Persians, Assyrians, Chaldeans, Syrians, Jews
- ◇ c) Settle in the Middle East, Asia
- ◇ 3) Japeth
- ◇ a) Japeth blessed by Noah (Ge 9:26)
- ◇ b) Japeth's descendants: Gauls (France), Scythians, Medes, Greeks, Iberes (Iberian Peninsula -Spain & Portugal)
- c) Settle in Europe
- ◇ E) Josephus' account — *historian (Jewish) 2000 yrs ago*
- ◇ 1) Names of places and people groups changed by Alexander the Great
- ◇ 2) Still places (in 75 A.D.) where the names date back to Noah

Timeline

Though no one knows for sure when the Flood occurred, we can look at the date of the rise of ancient civilizations to get a ballpark estimate for the Flood. Most history books show that the explosion of ancient civilizations along the Fertile Crescent takes place beginning about 3,000 B.C. Dating archaeological finds is not an exact science, though some in the scientific community would not admit that.

➜ On your timeline, locate the Flood at approximately 3,500 B.C.

Research & Reporting:

- Research the powerful and devastating impact of floodwaters. If there has been a local community that has recently experienced flooding, interview someone who experienced it first hand.

- Read and report on cavitation and its danger at hydroelectric dams.

- Research the requirements for ship stability in the water. Buoyancy is an important scientific principal that allowed the Ark to float. Write (include drawings) a description of the engineering and construction techniques required to build the Ark.

- Read and report on the theories concerning how deep the water was at the Flood. Was it above Mt. Everest, or was Mt. Everest not even there yet?

- Animal husbandry would have been a necessary science on the ark. Find out some of the requirements for caring for reptiles, birds, mammals, or others. Report your findings in a journalistic style.

- In the library or on the Internet, research any information about the mountains of Ararat and the search for Noah's Ark. Also, compare the varying opinions of the creationists concerning where they believe Noah's Ark is located.

- Find one of the books listed on the first page of this unit, along with the other history resource books for basic information on the location of the descendants of Ham, Shem and Japeth.

- Research the life of Noah in the Scriptures. Write a report about his life and the effect of his obedience to God.

Vocabulary

gopher wood	Shem	pitch	Japeth
cavitation	Ham	diluvial	cubit
antediluvian	vineyard	catastrophic	agriculture
buoyancy	hostility	uniformitarianism	ark
animal husbandry	flood	rebellion	altar
covenant	rainbow	descendant	

Hands On!

Maps
and
Mapping

- Using an atlas, encyclopedia or other resource, locate the mountains of Ararat on a map. (**Hint:** Look at Turkey, north of the Tigris and Euphrates rivers, southeast of the Black Sea.)

- On a clean worksheet map of the world, draw a small boat or use a sticker to indicate where the ark landed. Lightly shade the Black Sea with blue and black.

- Next, shade in the area where Ham, Shem and Japeth's descendants first settled with a separate color for each (use a study Bible for reference). What are the modern names for the countries in these areas?

- What is the capital city, religion, population, major exports, and type of government in these modern countries? What is the status of Christian outreach to them?

- Consult a relief map to discover the terrain of the mountains of Ararat. Is it desert, forest, swamp, coastal? Is it geologically active (any volcanoes)? What type of climate is typical in that part of the world? How would the terrain and climate have affected the reestablishment of mankind, agriculture, etc. How was it suitable for God's purposes?

 ## Arts in Action

- Try making an Easy-to-Make Noah's Ark by Dover.

- Make a boat: carve a soap boat, use Legos to construct a big boat, model wooden boat, raft-size houseboat (a good backyard project!)

- Start a year-long project carving animals. Check in the library or with a local expert (perhaps your grandfather?) for how-to information.

Art Appreciation

- If possible, locate a copy of Poortvliet's book, Noah's Ark:
  Do these paintings and sketches reflect what the Bible describes?
  How do they differ from your own impression of these historic events?
  After observing the paintings, try to draw or paint these same scenes:
  1) imitating Poortvliet (trace, follow colors, etc.)
  2) creating your own picture - draw individual "snapshots" of each of the
     animals (don't forget baby dinosaurs!)

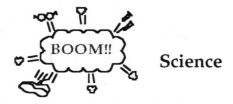 **Science**

- Create a "flood in a bottle" by putting sand, dirt, leaves, grass, and water in a tall
  glass jar with a lid. Shake vigorously and observe the settling process. Do you
  see how different layers can be formed very quickly? (Read **Dry Bones & Other
  Fossils** by Dr. Gary Parker.)

- Build a nice big sandbox dam and fill a big reservoir behind it. Watch the valleys
  it forms after you poke a hole in the dam.

- Plant a grape vine (if not possible, try potting a fruit vine or bush like raspberries,
  strawberries, etc.) Go on a field trip to a vineyard. Learn about the cultivation of
  grapes. Learn about fermentation. Rather than making wine, try drying grapes to
  make raisins, or make vinegar.

- Create a town of sand in the sandbox, then flood it with the hose. Notice the
  shapes and structures that wash away first, and the ones that last the longest.

 **Cooking**

Apricots have an interesting history. They seem to have been transplanted in
the Middle East during the time of Noah! This is a fun recipe (though I'm not sure
they had blenders on the Ark!)

Apricot Whip

1 pound dried apricots	1/2 tsp. almond extract
2 1/2 cup water	1 1/2 cup. heavy cream
1/2 tsp salt	1/2 cup sugar

Cook apricots in water & salt til tender (20 min.). Stir in sugar and flavoring. Puree
in blender. Chill. Beat cream till stiff, fold into apricots, chill again. Serves 6

Music

O F F
T H E
W A L L
! ! ! ! !

Sing this silly song:

The Lord told Noah there's gonna be a floody, floody
The Lord told Noah there's gonna be a floody, floody
Get those animals out of the muddy, muddy -
Children of the Lord.

Chorus: *So, rise and shine and give God the glory, glory*
Rise and shine and give God the glory, glory
Rise and shine and give God the glory, glory -
Children of the Lord.

Noah, he built him, he built him an arky, arky (repeat)
Built it out of gopher barky, barky -
Children of the Lord.

The animals they came on, they came on by twosies, twosies   (repeat)
Elephants and kangaroosies, roosies -
Children of the Lord.

It rained and poured for forty daysies, daysies (repeat)
Nearly drove those animals crazy, crazy -
Children of the Lord

The sun came out and dried up the landy, landy (repeat)
Everything was fine and dandy, dandy -
Children of the Lord

The animals they came off, they came off by threesies, threesies (repeat)
Elephants and chimpanzeesies, - zeesies -
Children of the Lord

And that is the end of, the end of our story, story (repeat)
Everything was hunky-dory, -dory -
Children of the Lord

- **Try this:** Listen to the music found in nature: the birds' song, the melodic tone of wind, the rhythm of falling rain... If you have a tape recorder, try to capture some of these sounds (and others) on tape - a symphony of nature!

- **Listen:** Many composers have created a **tone poem** or **symphonic poem** where a scene is conveyed through the music. (One of our favorites is **Pictures at an Exhibition** by Modeste Mussorgsky. If you can find this recording, listen especially to "The Ballet of the Baby Chicks in Their Shells." Another wonderful example of a symphonic poem type of music is Beethoven's **Sixth Symphony "Pastoral."**)

Idea Time!

Creative Writing

- Write a creative description of what the new world looked like after the Ark was opened and the people came out.

- Write a first person account of life on the Ark, from the viewpoint of a seasick giraffe.

- Write a book for young children describing Noah, the Ark and the Flood.

- You are a newspaper reporter for the "Enoch Free News." Your assignment is to interview Noah about this monstrosity he's building, and to write up his story for the newspaper feature, "Truth is Stranger Than Fiction."

- Finish this limerick about Cain:
  "There once was a man from Nod,
  Who offered his vegies to God..."

Art

- Illustrate the book for young children listed above.

- Design the T-shirt front and back, with logo and catchy saying, which Noah and his family would have worn to family reunions in years after the Flood.

- The possibilities for cartoons on this subject are almost endless!

Drama

- Reenact Noah and his family getting the animals on the Ark. Use your imagination to create props, sets and costumes. Be sure to include realistic sounds!

- Do a humorous skit about Noah's excitement when he realized the flood waters were receding. Variation: Show the animals' excitement!

The Big Picture

- Plan a presentation to your family, church, school, or neighbors of what you have learned about the cause of Noah's Flood, and how you have applied the lessons learned to your own life.

Unit Three

The Rise of Civilizations

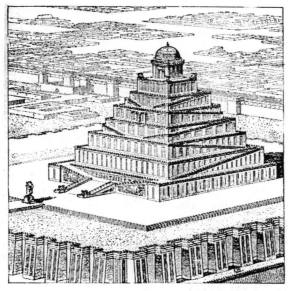

Ziggurat of Ur

Unit Objectives:

- to understand the ways and means, the uses and limits of archaeology;

- to investigate the sudden emergence of advanced civilizations in the archaeological record;

- to comprehend why God called Abraham out of Ur;

- to learn the myriad details and engineering demands required to build and sustain cities;

- to research the impact of the Tower of Babel on human history (i.e. languages, races, cultures);

- to become familiar with the geography and history of the Fertile Crescent.

Meet the People

- **The Holy Bible**
  Read Genesis 11 - 36; Psalm 105: 1-15; Romans 4; Galatians 3:5-14; Hebrews 11:8-21.

- **Then & Now** by Perring & Perring
  A fascinating look at the archaeological ruins of antiquity by two British archaeologists. This was the book that shows the ruins of Nimrud (in ancient Assyria), which was built originally by Nimrod! Includes several civilizations that we will be studying in this study guide. Each picture of an ancient site is accompanied by a full color overlay depicting how that place would have looked in its prime. **Great for the family!**

- **Kingfisher Illustrated History of the World**
  This is the best resource book for world history that we've seen. Though offered by a secular publisher, it is an excellent tool for seeing the "big picture" in history. **Upper elem and up.**

- **Usborne's Book of World History**
  A reference-style picture book of world history, this is a great resource book for younger children. **Early elementary.**

- **City Planning in Ancient Times** by Richard Currier
  This book shows the high level of city planning found in even the earliest civilizations. It is a very good introduction to what goes into planning cities. **Upper Elem. and up.**

- **Street Smart! Cities of the Ancient World**
  Another book showing how well planned many of the cities of antiquity were. Fascinating reading! **Elementary and up.**

- **Dig This! How Archaeologists Uncover Our Past** by Michael Avi-Yonah
  This a great introduction to the ways and means of archaeologists. It has lots of pictures of archaeological digs, which is tremendously helpful in trying to understand what a dig is really like. **Elementary and up.**

- **Digging to the Past: Excavations in Ancient Lands** by W. John Hackwell
  This children's book has wonderful descriptions of excavating archaeological sites. Even if you can't find this book or the one listed above, try to find a child's book on archaeology so your family will be able to comprehend the incredible "detective work" that is necessary to decipher ruins. **Elementary and up.**

• **Treasures Under the Sand - Wooley's Finds at Ur** by Alan Honour
This is an incredible book if you can find it! It is a children's biography of Leonard Wooley, the man who began excavating Ur in 1922. (*Unfortunately, the author's worldview doesn't see the Bible as literal history, and so the chronologies and explanations of the Old Testament events in this book are mistaken.*) Even with this problem, I still recommend it. This is the book that describes, among other things, Wooley's work with T.E. Lawrence - Lawrence of Arabia - prior to WWI.
Upper Elem. and up.

• **Ancient Crete** by Frances Wilkins
A fascinating look at an ancient civilization that was not known until the early 1900's. The Minoans were a highly advanced people whose civilization flourished around 2900 B.C.
Upper Elem and up.

• **Dazzling! Jewelry of the Ancient World**
Jewelry is an art form, it involves advanced technology, is a form of economics and was seen to be valuable in the afterlife. For example, the ancient royal tombs in Ur, excavated by Leonard Wooley, were found to contain vast quantities of jewelry.
Elementary and up.

• **Gods, Graves and Scholars** by C. W. Ceram
Often listed as required reading for college-level archaeology, this is an absolutely riveting book describing the real-life adventures of archaeologists from the 1800's to the early 1900's. The author's worldview is not a Biblical worldview, but he unwittingly continues to relate astonishing evidences pointing to the inerrancy of the Bible! Wondering if this book was really interesting, I asked my junior and senior high boys to read it. They couldn't put it down!
Junior High and up.

• **Asia: A Christian Perspective** by Mary Ann Lind
Published by YWAM Publishing, this book is filled with information about Asia. Though our main focus in this study guide is the rise of civilization in the Fertile Crescent, Egypt and Greece, there are many other early civilizations found in the archaeological record. What I found particularly helpful about this book was the historical background of some of these civilizations such as India and China. This book tells about the rise of Confucianism, Hinduism, and Buddhism - a significant part of understanding Asian cultures and early Asian civilizations. See **Resource List** for ordering info.
Junior High and up.

• **Strongholds of the 10-40 Window** edited by George Otis, Jr.
Published by YWAM Publishing, this is an intercessor's guide to the world's least evangelized nations. It includes basic facts, historical background, Christian outreach and specific prayer requests from resident Christians. This book will help you turn the head knowledge to heart compassion as you pray for the nations.
Great for the family!

• **SimCity**, for computers
A fascinating computer game which teaches the many areas one must necessarily consider in constructing a city.

Talk Together

- Listen to What in the World's Going on Here?, Tape One. What was the most interesting aspect to you of the rise of civilizations? Why? What questions do you have about this time period that you would like to learn more about? **History Journal:** Write those questions down, and as you study more material, write the answers to your questions. Write short bios of the interesting people. Illustrate the bios.

- Why do you think civilization seems to just "pop" onto the archaeological scene? What would have been necessary for humanity to rebuild cities, reestablish metal working, etc.?

- Do you think it was difficult for Abraham to leave Ur? Why or Why not? Why do you suppose that he later thought God needed help fulfilling the promise of an heir? What are the consequences even today of Abraham's momentary lack of trust?

- In your life, what examples are there of times when it was easy to trust God and times when it was difficult? What can we learn from Abraham's life? **History Journal:** Write your thoughts about this. Remember, we can learn a lot from other people's mistakes!

- Find out about the climate, terrain and political situation of the Fertile Crescent during the time of Abraham. How would you describe (specifically) the changes in his life and situation after he left Ur?

- What can you discover about the city of Ur in regards to their religious practices? Why do you think God called Abraham out of Ur?

- After reading the recommended scriptures, look in a Bible handbook or commentary to discover more information. Where is Ur located? Where is Canaan located? Where is Egypt located?

- One of the things that sets the Bible apart from other religious books is that it describes people accurately - with all of their failures and faults as well as their successes. Why do you think the Scriptures tell us that Abraham was a friend of God?

- What do you think is necessary to plan and build a city? Read about Nimrod, the great-grandson of Noah. He was a prolific builder of cities. Three of the cities he built have been located by modern day archaeologists: Babel (Babylon), Calah (Nimrud) and Ninevah. Discuss your findings, contrasting the Biblical description of early advancements with the evolutionary view of man's early history.

1804
1875

Teaching Time!

Seminar Outline

◇ III. Rise of Civilizations
◇   A) Tower of Babel
◇   1) Rebellion of man (Genesis 11:4-6) *Wishes to go to heaven*
◇   *to spread* 2) Dispersion of peoples by family and language groups *God wishes man*
◇   B) Three of the earliest civilizations from the archaeological record
◇ *3000 bc* (1) Sumerian
◇   2) Egyptian   *Joseph, slave to royalty* *x*
◇   3) Assyrian
◇   C) Different races in the human family
◇   1) Isolated gene pools
◇   2) Statistically - very fast changes

Joseph to Egypt

Timeline

→ Research the dates for the Sumerian, Egyptian, Assyrian, Minoan, Hittite, and Ebla civilizations. Then mark them on your timeline.

Research & Reporting:

• Find one of the books listed at the beginning of this unit, along with the encyclopedia or other history resource book for basic information on early civilizations. Key concerns will be: their location, appearance, religion, writings.

• Research and report on what structural requirements are necessary in order to build a city. (Water, sewer, residences, roads, etc.) Then consider the technology required to accomplish building those structures.

• Try to discover what archaeologists know about the size of Nimrod's cities.

• In the library, or on the Internet, research the Great Pyramid, the Ziggurat of Ur, and the Pyramid of the Sun in Mexico. Report on your findings, answering these questions: What are the similarities between these three structures?
                        What are some possible explanations of the similarities?

• Look in the library for the books by Thor Heyerdahl, especially Ra.

• Research the major language "families." Make a chart showing these language groups and their location in the world. What can you infer from this about the source, relationships, spread, and development of languages?

• Contact Institute for Creation Research in California to request information about the genetic and statistical explanation for the different races of man.

• Using the books listed on archaeology (or others), research what archaeologists can determine about a civilization based on the ruins, and what they cannot.

• List all of the tools, supplies, equipment and special needs an archaeology team must assemble before attempting an excavation.

• The Chronology of Archaeology on the following page lists dates and names. Research the events listed and report your findings.

• Read Unlocking the Mysteries of Creation (and others) about the unreliability of carbon dating. Research what methods archaeologists used, prior to the use of carbon dating, to determine the dates of various layers of ruins. Report your findings.

• In Scripture, discover the position of Abraham in regards to God's plan of redemption. Make a chart showing the flow of redemption from Adam to Abraham, Abraham to Jesus.

• Research and report on the "Rise and Fall of the Sumerian Civilization."

• Investigate the history of the Fertile Crescent from the time of Abraham to the present. Report your findings as if you were a newspaper reporter. (Journalism)

• Research the rise of civilizations in the Indus Valley and China. Compare and contrast these civilizations with the civilizations in the Fertile Crescent.

• Discover the level of mathematical proficiency in early civilizations. (**Hint:** What was used for money? for calculating? for astronomy?)

→ **Did you know?**
  During the excavation of Ur, a clay tablet was discovered with a mathematical theorem very similar to the Pythagorean theorem? Check it out!

Vocabulary

Fertile Crescent	antiquity	engineering	Tower of Babel
Sumer	civilization	dispersion	clay tablet
Ur	architecture	ziggurat	cuneiform
archaeology	carbon dating	babble	excavation
nation	city		

Chronology of Archaeology

Date	Name	Place
1760's	Karsten Niebuhr	Persepolis - Brought back bricks with cuneiform - His book was what Napoleon used on his trip to Egypt
1798	Napoleon/Denon	Egypt - First drawings of Upper & Lower Nile Dhautpoul - found Rosetta Stone, hieroglyphs
1802	Denon	Book Published
1802	Grotefend	German school teacher, first to understand how to decipher cuneiform
1821	Champollion	French scholar, deciphered Rosetta Stone
1837 1843	Henry Rawlinson "	English soldier, copied Behistun inscriptions Translates inscriptions (Old Persian, Babylonian, Elamite)
1843 - 46	Paul Emile Botta	French consul, first to discover Assyria - Khorsabad, palace of Sargon II
1845+ 1849+	Austen Layard "	British (French born) adventurer, uncovered Nimrud (biblical Calah) Uncovers Ninevah (Father of Assyriology)
1868+ 1876+	Heinrich Schliemann "	Uncovered Troy (against all odds) Uncovered Mycenae (Agamemnon? - Opposed Troy)
1899-1913	Robert Koldewey	Excavated Babylon, discovered Ishtar Gate, walls of Babylon, Hanging Gardens, and perhaps the Tower of Babel
1900-26	Sir Arthur Evans	British, uncovered Minoan civilization (predecessor to Mycenaean civ.) - Palace of Knossos
1927+	Leonard Wooley	Uncovered Ur of Abram
1964	Paolo Matthiae of Rome University	Uncovered Ebla (contemporary civilization of Sumer and Egypt)

Hands On!

Maps
and
Mapping

- Using an atlas, encyclopedia or other resource, locate Ur, Sumer, Egypt, Canaan, Assyria, Crete, China,and the Indus Valley on a map.

- Using a blank worksheet map of Europe and the Middle East, draw in the Tigris and Euphrates rivers, and lightly shade the Fertile Crescent in green. Draw and label the boundaries of the modern nations occupying this area. Are any of these nations named in the Bible? Place Sumer (Ur), Egypt, Canaan, Assyria, and Crete on your map. Trace Abraham's route from Ur to Egypt to Palestine.

- Consult a relief map to discover the terrain of the Fertile Crescent. Is it desert, mountain, forest, swamp, coastal? What type of climate is typical in that part of the world? How would the terrain and climate have effected this area and God's purpose for it?

- Make a papier maché relief map of this area. Where are the mountains located? The rivers? The seas? The trade routes? The cities? Also, identify the natural resources and ecosystems. (Get a library book on papier maché techniques.)

- Place Ninevah, Nimrud and Babylon on the map. What countries (both ancient and modern) are they located in?

- What is the name of the country or countries that today occupy the same area as Sumer, Egypt, Canaan, Assyria, Crete? What is the capital city, religion, population, major exports, and type of government in each modern country? What is the status of Christian outreach to these countries?

 **Arts in Action**

• Construct a small city from Legos, playdough, cardboard, etc. Where are the utilities? the parks? the transportation routes, the city/government center, the homes, the places of worship?

• Make a **fresco**: First, draw a simple design on paper. Next, on a separate piece of paper, repeat the design and color it with the colors you'd like to use for the fresco. Stir up a thick batch of Plaster of Paris, then cover a small board with a 1/4" layer of plaster. Smooth it over, then while it is still wet, trace the outlined design, the first paper, onto the plaster. Paint the design before the plaster dries. Be sure to use enough paint so that it is fairly thick. Let dry overnight. (**Hint:** If you have Visual Manna's **Teaching History Through Art**, you will find more information on this art form.)

• Make a clay pot! Find a book or an expert who can get you started with the simplest method - the coil pot. Consult the book (or expert) for needed items.

• Try making a **mosaic**: There are many different kinds of materials to choose from in making mosaics. *Archaeological digs have uncovered beautiful mosaics made from colored tiles. (Learn about the "Royal Standard of Ur.")*
For this project you can make a mosaic using colored bits of colored paper or tiles glued to wood. Start with an outline for your design, then glue the pieces of paper within the outline. Check out the library for more information on how to create this art form. (**Hint:** See **Teaching History Through Art** for more ideas.)

Art Appreciation

• If possible, find this painting:
    Tower of Babel
    by Pieter Bruegel, the Elder

Does the painting reflect what the Bible describes?
How does the painting differ from your own impression of this event?
After observing the painting, try to draw or paint this same scene:
    1) imitating Bruegel (trace, follow colors, etc.)
    2) creating your own picture

• Look for a photo of the royal headdress of Queen Pu-Abi of Ur.
Leonard Wooley found this amazing piece of jewelry while excavating the royal burial grounds in Ur. What does this show you about the culture of Ur? The craftsmanship of the time?

• Look for a photo of the artwork at the Minoan palace of Knossos at Crete.
What does this show you about the artistry and ability of the Minoan culture?

Music

Though evolutionists believe that the advanced technology and complexity needed for musical instruments would require music to develop long after earliest man, the archaeological record does not show this. In fact, exquisite harps were discovered in the royal tombs of Ur, and archaeologists now know that there were also drums and double reed instruments in this early civilization.

- **Try this:** Find a book in the library (or an instrument maker) who can show you how to construct a simple instrument: a drum, a bamboo flute, a whistle, a harp. (**Hint:** An excellent resource book to have in your personal library is the **Bible Time Crafts f for Kids,** by Neva Hickerson. She shows you numerous instruments to make, biblical clothes, jewelry, baskets and more.)

Cooking

The Fertile Crescent was a remarkably productive area for crops. Located between the two great rivers, the Tigris and Euphrates, the Fertile Crescent was occasionally flooded, which brought rich, wonderful soil for the farmers. Here is a recipe that is typical of Middle East cooking.

Lentils with tomatoes

1 cup brown lentils	1 tsp ground cumin
2 tbsp. oil	1/2 cup beef broth
1 large onion, minced	4 tomatoes, peeled and chopped
2 cloves garlic, minced	Salt & pepper

Soak lentils in cold water for 3 hours. Drain, then place lentils in pot of boiling salted water and cook over medium heat 30 min. Drain, reserve. Heat oil in large saucepan. Add onions and garlic, sauté about 5 minutes. Stirring constantly, add cumin and cook over high heat for 2 minutes. Add broth and lentils. Mix, then simmer, uncovered, over low heat until lentils are almost tender (15 minutes.) Stir in tomatoes and season. Continue simmering until tomatoes are tender, about 15 minutes. Serve immediately. Serves 4.

Idea Time!

Creative Writing

- Have each family member learn a few words in a separate foreign language - then try to communicate using these words that no one else understands! (A very small taste of the confusion at the Tower of Babel.)

- At the Tower of Babel, what would have been the impact of the sudden emergence of many different languages? Be a newspaper reporter at the Tower just after God confused the languages. Write the fast-breaking story!

- Write a short story about the farewell party in Ur for Abraham's family.

- You are one of the archaeological team working with Leonard Wooley in 1922. Write a letter home to your church family describing the discovery of Abraham's hometown.

- Write a "then and now" skit: Abraham leaves Ur while Leonard Wooley discovers Ur.

- Compose a song entitled, "Cities are Popping Up All Over!"

Drama

- Put on a puppet show describing Abraham and Sarah's adventures.

- Act out the discovery of Ur in 1922. Use your imagination to create props, sets and costumes. Be sure to show Mr. Wooley's excitement when he discovers it!

- Do a humorous skit about archaeologists sifting through a garbage dump that is 4,000 years old.

The Big Picture

- How can you present what you've learned about the rise of civilizations? Come up with a plan for how to share with your family, church, support group, school, or neighbors this exciting look at God's grace in dealing with men and nations.

Unit Four

Egypt and the Exodus

Unit Objectives:

- to understand the ancient Egyptian culture in light of God's dealings with it;

- to apply what is learned about Joseph's life - God intended it for good;

- to be familiar with the climate, terrain and location of Egypt, the Sinai Peninsula, the land of Midian;

- to examine the technical developments of ancient Egypt in science and math;

- to understand the miraculous, historical deliverance of the children of Israel out of the land of the Egyptians.

Meet the People

- **The Holy Bible**
  Read the book of Exodus; Genesis 12:10; Genesis 39 - 50; Deuteronomy 32-34; Psalms 66, 78, 95, 105, 136; Isaiah 19 -25, Ezekiel 29 -32; Acts 7:1-46; Hebrew 11:23-29.

- **Pyramid** by David Macauley
  An incredible look at the construction of a pyramid - you actually get the sense that you are inside a pyramid with the workers!   **Great for the family!**

- **Growing Up in Ancient Egypt** by Rosalie David
  This is an excellent introduction to the many facets of living in ancient Egypt. Though it is written for children, the information and layout makes it valuable to all ages. **Elementary.**

- **Mara, daughter of the Nile** by Eloise McGraw
  Riveting historical fiction! This is a wonderful way to make the ancient Egyptians, the political intrigues, and the places of power come to life.   **Upper elem and up.**

- **The Golden Goblet** by Eloise McGraw
  We really like this author! This book focuses on the intrigue and mystery of one orphaned boy's life. Another exciting means of making ancient Egypt come alive! **Upper elem and up.**

- **Tut's Mummy Lost and Found** by Judy Donnelly
  For elementary students, this book shows the fascinating adventure of Howard Carter who found King Tut in 1922.   **Elementary.**

- **The Cat of the Bubastes** by G. A. Henty
  Out of print, soon to be reprinted.Historical fiction at its best: includes Moses! **Jr High - up.**

- **Celebrate the Feasts** by Martha Zimmerman
  This book is filled with the why's and how-to's of celebrating the feasts of Israel.
  We learned so much about the meaning of the Last Supper, and the incredible picture of the Messiah depicted in the feast of Passover from this book - which also shows *how* to celebrate this and the other feasts.   **Great for the family!**

- **Make it Work! Ancient Egypt** by Andrew Haslam & Alexandra Parsons
  This is one of a series of the most incredible hands-on books of projects I've ever seen! It shows how to construct clothing, make jewelry, create instruments, even make a chariot! See resource list for ordering info.   **Great for the family!**

- **The Riddle of the Rosetta Stone: Key to Ancient Egypt** by James Cross Giblin
  An absolutely fascinating book about the man who deciphered the Rosetta Stone.
  Great for the family!

- **The Mountain of Moses: The Discovery of Mount Sinai** by Larry Williams
  Out-of-print. If you can find a copy, this is a fascinating book detailing the problems associated with the traditional site of Mt. Sinai, the problem of where the Israelites crossed over the Red Sea, and more. It not only details the problems, it offers a solution. **Jr. High-up.**

- Video: **The Ten Commandments**   **Good for the family!**

Talk Together

• Listen to What in the World's Going on Here?, Tape One. What was the most interesting aspect to you of the events in Egypt and the Exodus which were mentioned? Why? What questions do you have about this time period that you would like to learn more about?

History Journal: Write those questions down, and as you study more material, write the answers to your questions. Write short bios of the interesting people. Illustrate the bios.

• Why do you think God allowed Joseph to be taken as a slave to Egypt? Are God's purposes always clear to us in difficult situations? Why couldn't He have made an easier path for Joseph to walk? What can we learn through this person's life about the character and ways of God? "You intended it for evil but God intended it for good."

History Journal: Write in your history journal about the lessons of Joseph's life, and the amazing way God used him in history.

• What can you discover about the Egyptian culture in regards to their treatment of other peoples? Were they warlike people? What evidence supports your answer?

• Why do you think that Moses chose to identify with the Jews who were now slaves in Egypt, rather than to enjoy the pleasures of Pharaoh's court? What did Moses say to God at the burning bush in the wilderness? Why do you think he was so hesitant to be God's mouthpiece?

• Did God love both the descendants of Jacob and the Egyptians? Why do you think so? (**Hint:** He demonstrated His power to those given over to false idol worship.)

• The ten plagues of Egypt have been described as the toppling of each of the Egyptian sacred deities, which would have demonstrated to the Egyptians as well as to the Israelites that Jehovah God was the true God. Why would God want the Egyptians to know this?

• Why were the ancient Egyptians so concerned about the afterlife? What are some of the ways they demonstrated their concern? What scientific techniques of the Egyptians are a mystery to us?

• As you learn more about Egypt in further studies, remember that God kept sending those who knew Him into this land to demonstrate His character and power. Why would He do that?

• After reading the book of Exodus, look in a Bible handbook or commentary to discover more information. Where is Egypt located? Where is the land of Midian located? Locate all of the water surface that comprises the Red Sea. Where does Galatians 4:25 say that Mount Sinai is?

Discover Noah's Ark
—Ron Wyatt

Larry Williams

Teaching Time!

Seminar Outline

◊ IV. Egypt and God's interaction with them
◊   A) God's promise to Abraham (Ge 15:13)
◊   "Then He said to Abram: "Know certainly that your descendants will be strangers in a land that is not theirs, and will serve them and they will afflict them four hundred years."
◊   B) Joseph, the Architect of Egypt
◊   1) Entered Egypt approximately 1875 B.C. (died c 1800 B.C.)
◊   2) Exodus 1:6-8
◊   "And Joseph died, all his brothers, and all that generation. But the children of Israel were fruitful and increased abundantly, multiplied and grew exceedingly mighty; and the land was filled with them. Now there arose a new king over Egypt, **who did not know Joseph.**"
◊   C) Moses and the Exodus
◊   1) Moses raised as royalty *w/ the pharoah*
◊   2) The crossing of the Red Sea

Sinai? in Arabia? Saudi

Egypt Golden Age —time in New Kingdom with "good pharohs" at the end of Golden age Thuickmos II —died young 1499 BC

Ocenatan— sun God l wife Nefretiti ↓ son was King Tut ? died Ε ? (death angel passover?)

Timeline

   The Exodus is thought by many to have occurred approximately 1435 B.C. There are others who believe that the Exodus took place much later, in the 1200's B.C. According to Genesis 15:13 ,the descendants of Abraham were going to be slaves in a land not theirs for 400 years. Many scholars place Joseph's entry into Egypt at about 1875 B.C.. Therefore, the 1435 B.C. date is more in keeping with the four hundred years of slavery prophesied.

   The difficulty in pinpointing dates and Pharaohs lies with the Egyptian chronologies. When we look back in history, we often expect to find a "digital clock" running, showing the exact moment an event occurred. Unfortunately, especially in ancient civilizations, that is not the case. Instead, there are many educated guesses about the time frame in which certain key events and players happened. In fact, a significant shift in the dates of Egyptian dynasties has just recently occurred which completely changes the understanding of who was what and where, when! When it comes to the Exodus, this guesswork is even more pronounced since the Egyptians seem to have left out of their official records anything that made them look like losers. And in this contest, Moses and the God of Moses were certainly the winners.

➔ On your timeline, mark the possible dates of the Egyptian dynasties. Now, mark the Exodus where your research suggests.

Research & Reporting:

• Research and explain what hieroglyphic writing is, and how it was deciphered in modern times. (**Hint:** Look up the Rosetta Stone and Jean François Champollion.)

• Research and report on the use of triangulation in surveying ancient Egypt. Why was regular surveying required? Is triangulation still used in surveying?

• Compile a list of names, dates and accomplishments of Egypt's dynasties. How does this list compare with the events listed in the Bible (as far as we can tell)?

• In the library, or on the Internet, research any information related about Egypt. (Newspapers, magazines, books, videos)

• Investigate the history of Egypt from the earliest times to the present. Report your findings as if you were a newspaper reporter. (Journalism)

• Compare and contrast the history of Egypt and the history of Israel. What cultural distinctives (i.e. religion, war, politics, class structure) continue in each nation throughout the centuries?

• Summarize the factors that led to Egypt's far- reaching dominion and the factors leading to their decline. Be sure to include the impact of the Nile.

• Research the life of Joseph in the Scriptures; the life of Moses.

• Read Exodus and note the geographical descriptions of the flight from Egypt, the crossing of the Red Sea, the route to, and depiction of Mt. Sinai (reference Gal. 4:25 also.) Next, find a description of the traditional site of Mt. Sinai and the Sea of Reeds. Do these sites conflict with the biblical text?
(**Hint:** Look for water and vegetation at traditional Mt. Sinai, room to camp at the base of the mountain for at least 600,000 people, information about artifacts or any other telltale signs of 600,000 people camping at the traditional Mt. Sinai, location of Egyptian turquoise and copper mines on the Sinai Peninsula, etc.) Write a report explaining what you discover.

• Find one of the books listed at the beginning of this unit, along with the encyclopedia or other history resource book for basic information on what would be needed in a hot, dry climate to sustain life for people, flocks and herds. Is it available on the Sinai Peninsula? Would it be available in the land of Midian? Make a chart listing the necessary requirements to sustain life, and show which of these requirements are fulfilled in each of these two locations.

- Research and report on the weather conditions and ecosystems in Egypt and in Midian. How would this have impacted the children of Israel as they wandered for forty years?

- Compare and contrast the desert in Egypt with other deserts, such as the Sahara or Mojave. How did the Nile River impact the desert of ancient Egypt? How is this different today?

- Learn more about nomadic desert dwellers (like the Bedouins), their lifestyle and how they care for their animals. Write a report showing the lifestyle of the desert dweller, then what we can extrapolate from this in regards to the Israelites in the wilderness.

11/15/04
A →
- Investigate the book of Exodus in the Old Testament. To whom did God speak? What were the messages? How did the people (both Egyptian and Israelite) respond? How did God deal with each of them?

- Read Exodus 12. Now, using either Celebrate the Feasts or another title describing the Jewish feast of Passover, chart the similarities between the historic event of Passover and the feast.

- Summarize, either in written or verbal form, what you know about:

  1) the importance of ancient Egypt;
  2) the enslavement and deliverance of the Israelites;
  3) the Exodus;
  4) the wilderness wandering.

Vocabulary

Moses	Midian	plague
Joseph	Goshen	famine
sorcerers	Nile River	slavery
magicians	Mt. Horeb	exodus
pharaoh	Mt. Sinai	quota
hieroglyphics	petroglyph	Passover
irrigation	triangulation	survey
pyramid		

Hands On!

**Maps
and
Mapping**

- Using an atlas, encyclopedia or other resource, locate Egypt, the Red Sea, and the land of Midian on a map.

- What is the name of the country or countries that today occupy the same area as Egypt and Midian? What is the capital city, religion, population, major exports, and type of government in each modern country? What is the status of Christian outreach to these countries?

- On a clean worksheet map, draw the boundaries of Egypt (including the area of their copper and turquoise mines), draw the Nile River, label the location of Memphis, Thebes, the Valley of the Kings. What modern day cities are close to these ancient cities?

- Take your family outside to demonstrate triangulation for them as you measure the yard or park or field. Look in the library for more info.

- Consult a relief map to discover the terrain of Egypt, the Sinai Peninsula, the land of Midian. Is it desert, mountain, forest, swamp, coastal? What type of climate is typical in that part of the world? How would the terrain and climate have affected the Egyptian culture and God's purpose for it?

 Arts in Action

- Try carving a Sphinx out of soap. (**Hint:** Make your own soap, then carve it - for a supplier of soap-making kits, see the Resource List.)

- Sketch a simple picture in the style of the Egyptian tomb paintings. Then make a dry plaster (**a secco**) painting: using very smooth plaster of Paris, brush a 1/8" layer of plaster over a piece of wood. When dry, lay your sketch over the wood and trace the outline with a nail. Use tempera to paint picture. Remember to keep it simple!

- Make a pyramid out of Legos, or other materials. How big is the Great Pyramid of Cheops? What is the average weight of each stone? How much, approximately, does the Great Pyramid weigh?

- Egyptians liked to use jewelry in adorning themselves. (This came in very handy when the Israelites took their back wages out of the country!) Find a library book, or a local expert, to show you how to make jewelry. There are many, many possibilities for materials, colors, size, shape!

Art Appreciation

- If possible, find this painting:
  The Deliverance of the Israelites
    by Bernardo Luini

- And, look for pictures of the tomb paintings of ancient Egypt.

  Do these paintings reflect what the Bible describes?
  How do the paintings differ from your own impressions?
  After observing the paintings, try to draw or paint these same scenes:
    1) imitating Luini, or the ancient Egyptian artists (trace, use colors, etc.)
    2) creating your own picture

 ## Music

In ancient Egypt, as in other early civilizations, people played various kinds of instruments, such as flutes, harps and drums. But they were not the only ones in Egypt with instruments! Exodus 15 tells us that Moses' sister, Miriam, played the timbrels (tambourine) during the triumphant song of deliverance after Pharaoh and his army were drowned in the Red Sea.

Have you ever listened to a tambourine? Sometimes it is played consistently and regularly on the beat, but sometimes the tambourine player will make different patterns: a long, held-out "shimmering" sound, or a series of short, quick taps. The performer is creating a pattern of sounds, some longer and some shorter.
Recite these children's verses:
"Pat-a-cake, pat-a-cake, Baker's man..."
"Twinkle, twinkle, little star..."
"Hot cross buns..."
Now, try clapping one of these verses for your family. Can anyone guess which pattern you are clapping? That pattern is called the **rhythm.**

One of the five elements of music, **rhythm** is the distinctive pattern of long and short notes in each piece of music. Along with the pattern of notes is the underlying pulse, or beat, of the music. The beat can be slow or fast or medium. We use the term **tempo** to mean the speed of music. So, slow music, like a lullaby, has a slow tempo, and fast music, like a march, has a faster tempo.

- **Try this!** Buy or make a tambourine, and play a rhythm like Miriam would have used.

Science

• Try making bricks: using water, clay soil, and straw, mix up a batch of "bricks." Make wooden rectangular forms to put the mixture into. Let it dry (it may take several days.) What's the difference between sun-dried brick and kiln-dried brick?

• Ancient Egyptians may have used levers and pulleys to build the pyramids. Construct a system of pulleys and ropes to try lifting a heavy object like a concrete block. Notice that the more pulleys used, the easier.   Consult the library for more info.

Cooking

Since this unit looks at two different people groups, the Egyptians and the Israelites who fled Egypt, we will make two different recipes. Do you remember what the children of Israel complained about in the wilderness in regards to good ol' Egyptian food? (You may want to listen to Keith Green's **"So You Wanna' Go Back to Egypt"**.) Sample the following and see what they were talking about! (Be sure NOT to complain!!)

Stewed Beef with Okra (Egyptian)

2 tbsp oil   1/2 tsp. ground coriander
2 tbsp butter   1 pound tomatoes, peeled & sliced
1 1/2 pound stew beef (or lamb) cubed   1 tbsp tomato paste
2 onions, chopped   2 10 oz. pkgs. frozen okra
2 cloves garlic, minced   Salt & pepper

Heat oil and butter in casserole. Add meat cubes & saute until brown. Add onions, garlic, coriander, fry for one minute. Add tomatoes, paste, seasoning. Cover stew with water, bring to boil, reduce heat, cover, simmer 1 hour. Add okra, cook 30 minutes more.

Unleavened Bread (The Exodus)

4 cups unbleached flour
1 tsp. salt
1 1/2 cup water, room temp.

Combine flour and salt. Add enough water to make a dough that will clean sides of bowl and gather into a ball. Turn out onto lightly floured surface, knead 10 minutes. Shape into ball and cut in half. Cut each half into 8 pieces and form into 16 balls. Roll out each ball to form about a 7 " circle. Place on ungreased baking sheet and bake in 500 degree oven for about 5 minutes. Makes 16.

Idea Time!

Creative Writing

- Write a fictional account of an Egyptian orphan who flees to a Hebrew family during the plagues, and comes with them on the Exodus.

- Be a newspaper reporter for the Palestine daily, "The Patriarch," and write the human interest story "Family Finds Long-Lost Son in Egypt."

- Write an acrostic poem from the Hebrew perspective describing the night of the first Passover.

- Discover the connection these words have to the unit, and then write a rhyming poem using them: *sea, flee, free*   *pharaoh, marrow, narrow*
  pulley, bully, fully   *flood, blood, mud*   *slave, brave, save*

- Imagine you were invited to a formal dinner at Nefertiti's palace. Write a detailed description of the guests, their outfits and the food served for the magazine, Lifestyles of the Rich Egyptians.

- Make a pun about Egypt. Like this:

    What do you call a pyramid that smells bad?
    A stynx!

Art
- As a political cartoonist, draw a cartoon for the "Mt. Sinai Herald," showing the confrontation between Pharaoh and Moses.

Drama

- Act out the Exodus. Use your imagination to create props, sets and costumes. Be sure to include realistic fear, as well as rejoicing! Add appropriate songs (such as "Pharaoh, pharaoh"), worship choruses ("Horse and Rider), etc.
- Do a humorous skit about Moses explaining to his wife that the reason he was late for dinner was because God was talking out of a burning bush!

The Big Picture

- Plan a Passover feast and invite friends. As you go through the feast, explain to your guests the significance of what is being done, and the historical background of the feast. Share about God's mercy and love to both the Egyptians and the Hebrews.

Unit Five

The Children of Israel

Altar of Incense

Unit Objectives:

- to understand the chronology of the kingdom of Israel;

- to comprehend the significance and the glory of Israel;

- to understand the reason for the divided kingdom and its impact on history;

- to know the terrain and strategic location of Israel, and God's purpose in setting His people there;

- to apply the lessons of Israel to our own lives.

Meet the People

• **The Holy Bible**
Read Joshua, Judges, Ruth, 1&2 Samuel, 1 Kings, 2 Kings 1 - 14, 1 Chronicles, 2 Chronicles 1-27, Psalms, Proverbs.

• **Halley's Bible Handbook**
This book contains wonderful study helps and insights related to the Old and New Testaments. It includes archaeological explanations from a Biblical perspective. (However, the archaeologists' findings in the Fertile Crescent are interpreted to mean that the Flood was a localized event.)
Upper elem and up.

• **The New Unger's Bible Handbook** revised by Gary Larson
This is my preferred source for information and insight on the archaeological record from a Biblical perspective. It is filled with color pictures, timelines, notes, helps, and exciting tidbits!
Upper elem and up.

• **Daily Chronological Bible**
Reading this Bible was our basic introduction to the concept of studying ancient civilizations and the Bible. It is set up chronologically with wonderful insights into the history of the Scriptures.
Great for the family!

• **Josephus** edited by Paul Maier
Since one of Josephus' purposes was to explain the history of Israel, this is an excellent (although difficult) resource for studying this subject.
High school and up.

• **A Family Guide to the Biblical Holidays** by Robin Scarlata and Linda Pierce
A wonderful resource for celebrating the feasts of Israel in your family. Many helpful ideas and suggestions - an excellent addition to this study.
Great for the family!

• **Bible Atlas**
Regardless of which one you choose, a Bible atlas is an indispensable tool in understanding the history of the children of Israel.
Great for the family!

• **Then and Now** by Perring and Perring
The ruins of ancient civilizations, including Israel, will come to life for your family as you see the artist's rendition of what it once looked like superimposed over the ruin that now exists. See Masada, Jerusalem and more!
Great for the family!

• **Sold! - The Origins of Money & Trade**
Economics and trade routes had a mighty impact on cultures from earliest times. Learn more about how this worked, and then apply it to the country of Israel.
Upper elem and up.

• Video Series: **That the World May Know** from Focus on the Family
Both an incredible introduction to the Holy Land and also valuable "faith lessons" from the history of this people. See Resource List for ordering info.
Great for the family!

Talk Together

- Listen to What in the World's Going on Here?, Tape One. What was the most interesting aspect to you of the events in Israel which were mentioned? Why? What questions do you have about this time period that you would like to learn more about?

  History Journal: Write those questions down, and as you study more material, write the answers to your questions. Write short bios of the interesting people. Illustrate the bios.

- After reading about the geography, climate, and political situation during the time of the conquest of Canaan and the kingdom of Israel, why do you think God chose that geographic location for His chosen people? (**Hint:** Consider trade routes.)

- Joshua was one of twelve men who had spied out the land promised by God to the children of Israel. But of the twelve, only Joshua and Caleb came back with an enthusiastic, God-fearing report. All of the others spoke glowingly of the natural resources but were terrified of the fierce people populating Canaan. They warned the people that if they tried to go into to the land, they would be destroyed. If you had been one of those delivered out of Egypt, what would you have said about this report? Why?

- After reading the book of Joshua, look in a Bible handbook or commentary to discover more information. Where is the Jordan river located? Where did the Israelites enter the land? Where is Jericho located? Why do you think God told the Israelites to march around Jericho? Who led the march; why; is this typical military strategy? How would you describe God's "military strategies"?

- Why do you think God commanded the various feasts of Israel?

- What can you discover about the Israelites in regards to their treatment of other peoples? Why would God instruct them to destroy the Canaanites? (**Hint:** Read Genesis 15:13-16.)

- Describe the period of the Judges of Israel. Why did the nation suffer so many difficulties?

- Read 1 & 2 Samuel. Describe the process of Israel's becoming a kingdom. Why do you think God told Samuel to anoint David as king? What can you learn from this about God's ways and methods?

- In the Psalms, David shares everything from dark despair to exultant victory. Match some of the events in David's life with the Psalms he wrote. What can we learn from David's example? Did David's attitude toward God make a difference in his situation? Why do you suppose David did not kill King Saul when he had the chance?

- Discuss King Solomon's reign. Why do you think he turned away from God after having received so much? How can we learn to apply this lesson in our own lives?

Teaching Time!

Seminar Outline

◇ V.   Kingdom of Israel
◇   A) Saul
◇   B) David
◇   C) Solomon
◇   1) Who was he?
◇   a) 1 Kings 4: 29 - 34
◇   2) What happened?
◇   a) Deut. 17:14-20
◇   b) 1 Kings 10:28- 11:13
◇   D) Divided Kingdom
◇   1) Reheboam (son)
◇   a) 1 Kings 12:13-14
◇   2) Jereboam (servant)
◇   a) 1 Kings11:37-38
◇   b) 1 Kings 12:26-28

Timeline

→   On your timeline, mark Joshua, the period of the conquest of Canaan and the Judges of Israel. The kings of the united Israel were King Saul, King David and King Solomon. Mark their reigns on the timeline, and then show when the kingdom divided. Using a good study Bible or handbook, mark the kings of the northern kingdom of Israel and the kings of the southern kingdom of Judah.

Research & Reporting:

• Find one of the books listed at the beginning of this unit, along with the encyclopedia or other history resource book for basic information on Israel.

• Compare and contrast Ruth and Rahab; Samson - Gideon; Samuel - Eli.

• Do a research paper with pictures on the differences between the northern kingdom of Israel and the southern kingdom of Judah. Include geographical, political, economic, and religious differences.

• Find out about the temple of Solomon. Write a report discussing the funding, the materials, the building of the temple, as well as the use or abuse of it in history.

• Discover the geographical boundaries of the neighboring countries (such as Phoenicia, Philistia, Moab, Edom, etc.) What part did Egypt play in the politics of the area during this time? Make a diagram showing the who, where, when, and how of these allies and enemies.

• Research and write about what archaeologists have uncovered in the digs of Jericho, Ebla, Jerusalem, Tell el Amarna and others.

• Research and report on the ancient trade routes of the Middle East. What modes of transportation were used in this area? What have archaeologists learned about trade goods imported and exported? What was used for money? How did this aspect impact Judah/Israel?

• Research and report on the consequences of obedience and disobedience in Israel's history.

• Investigate in the library, or on the Internet, the history of Israel from the time of Joshua to the present. Report your findings as if you were a newspaper reporter. (Journalism)

• Learn about Phoenicia: cities, export, navigation, trade routes, relation to Israel. What new process did the Phoenicians bring to writing? Hiram was king of Tyre during Solomon's reign. What did he do for Israel?

Vocabulary

conquest	temple	tabernacle	tribute
alliance	angel	monarchy	theocracy
prophet	anoint	Philistines	Jericho
Jerusalem	Jordan river	Gilgal	Gaza
Lachish	Canaan	idolatry	talent
shekel	Pentateuch	Talmud	Torah
tell (tel)	Ark of the Covenant		

Hands On!

**Maps
and
Mapping**

- Using an atlas, encyclopedia or other resource, locate Israel on a map. Consult a relief map to discover the terrain of Israel. Was it desert, mountain, forest, swamp, coastal? What type of climate is typical in that part of the world? Where are the mountain ranges? Where are the rivers? Where are the trade routes? (**Hint:** Remember to include Phoenicia.) What strategic geographic importance does this piece of land hold for Europe and Africa?

- What is the capital city, people groups, religion, population, major exports, and type of government in modern Israel? What is the status of Christian outreach?

- On a clean, empty map of Israel, draw the boundaries of the ancient kingdoms, show the rivers, mountains, deserts, valleys, etc. Label the location of Jericho, Jerusalem, Bethlehem, Tyre, Sidon and other cities listed in your readings.

- Using what you have learned about the terrain, construct a papier maché map of Israel showing the Mediterranean, Dead Sea, Sea of Galilee, Jordan river, Kidron Valley, Hinnom Valley, Desert of Zin, Desert of Paran, Desert of Shur, Plain of Sharon, Golan Heights, the mountain ranges, the neighboring countries and the important cities. Do your best - this will be something to use long term!

Arts in Action

- Try making Biblical costumes for your "reenacting" of Bible scenes. (I highly recommend the **Bible Time Crafts for Kids** by Neva Hickerson as it is filled with wonderful costumes, crafts, musical instruments, etc. that are easy to make!)

- Draw a picture of David, the shepherd. Can you depict David's Psalm 23 through art? What expression does the shepherd have on his face?

- The Phoenician exported a purple dye that was extraordinarily expensive (one drop of dye from each mollusk!) Try dying fabric using a natural source for dye. Check the library for info. (**Hint:** See **Teaching History Through Art** for more!)

• Make a model of the Tabernacle or Solomon's Temple. There are cut-out style Tabernacle kits available, or you could construct it from papier maché; fabric over a dowel; clay; bread dough... whatever works.

Art Appreciation

• If possible, find this painting:
    The Judgment of Solomon
        by Peter Paul Rubens

Does this painting reflect what the Bible describes?
How does the painting differ from your own impression of this historic time?
After observing the paintings, try to draw or paint these same scenes:
    1) imitating Rubens (trace, follow colors, etc.)
    2) creating your own picture

• Also, read carefully the description in Scripture of the artwork commanded by God for the Tabernacle, and the artwork used in Solomon's Temple. What does this tell you about the value God places on beauty, on artistic endeavors? **Field Trip:** Visit a fabric and a jewelry store to look at the colors, textures, etc. listed as being used in these two places dedicated to God.

 ## Music

The Bible is filled with references to musical instruments and singing in ancient Israel, both of which were used in the joyful worship of God. The Psalms were all meant to be sung. Many even have comments telling which instruments were to accompany! There were professional musicians employed in the worship at the Temple, and Scripture indicates that these musicians were to be skilled.

One of the most incredible stories in the Old Testament is found in 2 Chronicles 20:1-30. It tells of a very unique task for musicians - to go into battle, before the army, worshiping and praising God! Read this account out loud for the whole family, and then stand and sing together the Doxology:

Praise God from whom all blessings flow,
Praise Him all creatures here below,
Praise Him above ,ye heavenly host,
Praise Father, Son and Holy Ghost.

• **Try this:** Do you know any worship hymns or choruses using Psalms? Have each one in the family look through the Psalms, and when anyone recognizes the words to a familiar song, sing it. Some you may know: Psalm 125, Psalm 89, Psalm 63, Psalm 34.

• You may also want to try singing your own melody with a Psalm. This is one of my family's favorites (to the tune of "Short'ning Bread"):
    You have dealt well with Your servant,
    O Lord, according to Your word.   Psalm 119:65

Science

- **Field Trip:** Visit a farm with sheep, or a petting zoo. Ask lots of questions about the care of sheep, the way the wool is removed, what the wool can be used for. If you can touch the fleece, rub the wool in your fingers for a few minutes. What makes your fingers soft?

   Is there anyone spinning the wool? Ask if you may try it. (It's not as easy as it looks!) Is there anyone weaving the wool? Knitting? Crocheting? This is a great time to learn how to do any of these. Check the library for how-to books.

- Chemistry: Learn how grapes are grown, and then turned into wine. What is the process? Try an experiment with some type of fermentation.

Cooking

God told His chosen people that He was taking them to a land filled with milk and honey. In order to really understand how wonderful milk and honey are, we are going to make Yogurt Cake with Honey Frosting. Thank you, Lord!

Yogurt Cake & Honey Frosting

1 cup butter	3 cups flour
2 cups sugar	1/4 tsp salt
4 eggs, separated (room temp)	4 tsp. baking powder
1 cup yogurt (plain)	3 tsp. lemon extract

Cream butter and sugar together until light and fluffy. Add the egg yolks one at a time, beating until creamy and light. Stir in yogurt. Add flour, salt, baking powder, lemon extract. Mix well. Beat egg whites until stiff but not dry, and mix 1/3 into batter. Fold in remaining egg whites. Turn into a 10" tube pan and bake in preheated 350 degree oven for about 60 minutes, or until done.

Frosting:

1/2 cup honey	1/4 tsp salt
2 egg whites, room temp.	1/8 tsp cream of tartar

Bring honey to boil in saucepan. Beat egg whites until frothy, add salt and cream of tartar, continue to beat. When egg whites hold soft peaks, slowly add honey in a thin stream. Continue to beat until meringue is stiff and glossy. Frost cake when cool.

Idea Time!

Creative Writing

- Write a fictional account of an Israelite named "Benjamin the Skeptic" on the sixth and seventh day of the march around Jericho.

- In the style of David, compose a psalm of thanksgiving to God. (Psalm 100)

- Be a newspaper reporter for the "Desert Sun Times" and give the exclusive inside scoop on the spies who came back from Canaan.

- The Alphabet Game: Get your family together to play this game. One person starts with the letter "a." They must name a word that pertains to this unit beginning with "a" (such as "Ark of the Covenant".) The next person gives a word beginning with "b" (like "Benjamin"). Keep the game going through all of the letters. How did you do? (Variation: have each member of the family use the same letter, and then everyone advances to the next letter.)

- Finish this limerick about Hiram:
  "There was a great king from Tyre,
  Who sent out his craftsmen for hire..."

Drama

- Act out the story of the ten spies. Use your imagination to create props, sets and costumes. Be sure to include the results for the eight and the results for the two!
- Perform the scene with King David bringing the Ark to Jerusalem.
- Do a humorous skit about Gideon and his army.
- Write a script that highlights the most important events during these 600 years. Act it out using a narrator, worship songs, and quick scene changes.

Feast

- Learn about the Feast of Tabernacles. Make your Succoth booths outside, prepare festive food, and invite your family, friends, church over to help you celebrate God's wonderful provision. During this time, display your projects from this unit, sing the songs, perform the skits. Have a time of sharing how this new understanding has impacted and changed your life. Finally, pray for the people of Israel, for the peace of Jerusalem, and for our own nation.

Unit Six

Assyria and the Destruction of Israel

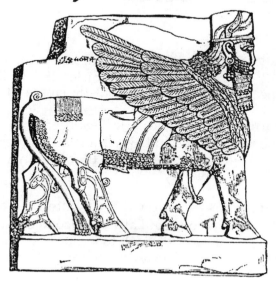

Winged Bull of Assyria

Unit Objectives:

- Understand the historical, geographical and cultural setting for the book of Jonah and the Assyrian civilization;

- Observe the reality of God's judgment upon the northern kingdom of Israel;

- Comprehend the significance of Judah's deliverance from the Assyrian siege;

- Recognize the historical fulfillment of the prophecies against Assyria;

- Appreciate the advanced accomplishments of this early civilization;

- Evaluate the impact of the discovery of Ninevah upon the Bible scoffers of the 1800's.

Meet the People

• **The Holy Bible**
Read the book of Jonah and Nahum who both prophesied to the Assyrians.
Also read Genesis 10:8-12; 2 Kings 15 - 19; 2 Chronicles 28 - 32:22; Isaiah 10:5-15; Isaiah 19:
23-25; Isaiah 36 - 38; Micah 5:5-6; Zephaniah 2:13-15; Hosea 11:1-12.

• **Secrets of the Royal Mounds** by Cynthia Jameson
This delightful book is the story of Austen Layard, a British adventurer in the mid-1800's,
who was the first to discover the cities of Assyria. It's certainly worth the trouble to find, as
it is written in a capture-your-interest style. **Great for the family!**

• **Discoveries Among the Ruins of Ninevah** by Austen Layard
This is a fascinating first-person account of Layard's second dig at Ninevah. It was
published in the mid-1800's, so may be difficult to locate, but again, it's certainly worth the
trouble. It mentions Jonah's tomb in Ninevah and more! Also look for any other titles by
Layard. **High school and up.**

• **Scrawl! Writing in Ancient Times**
One of the most amazing finds in the archaeological digs of Assyria was the library of
Asshurbanipal, containing 30,000 books! Learn more about early writing and the steps
involved in deciphering it using this and the following book. **Upper Elem and up.**

• **Ancient Scrolls** by Michael Avi-Yonah, retold by Richard Currier
This is a very interesting book about a fascinating subject. "The pen (or perhaps the stylus) is
mightier than the sword" has held true from the very beginning! **Junior High and up.**

• **Then and Now** by Perring and Perring
One chapter of this great archaeological resource deals with Nimrud (known
as Calah in the Bible) which was once the capital city of Assyria. **Great for family!**

• Video: **Assurnasirpal, The Assyrian King** The Anthony Roland Collection
Probably available through your state or university library, this is a fascinating video of the
Assyrians. One section is told from the viewpoint of Assurnasirpal, an Assyrian king. It
utilizes the sculptures and artistic carvings on the now uncovered palace walls to tell the
stories of the culture. The video may seem long to younger children, but the entire family will
benefit from seeing the surrounding terrain and amazing art. **Great for family!**

• **The Destruction of Sennacherib** by Lord Byron
A poem showing the power of the Lord over the Assyrians. **Great for family!**

Talk Together

- Listen to What in the World's Going on Here?, Tape One. What was the most interesting aspect to you of the events in Assyria which were mentioned? Why? What questions do you have about this time period that you would like to learn more about?

   History Journal: Write those questions down, and as you study more material, write the answers to your questions. Write short bios of the interesting people. Illustrate the bios.

- Imagine you were trying to share the truth of Scripture with someone in the 1800's. They scoff at you in derision and say, "The Bible couldn't possibly be true. Look at the way it describes empires like Assyria, which everyone knows never existed!" What would you say to that person after Austen Layard's discovery of Nimrud and Ninevah?

- After reading about the climate, terrain and political situation during the time of Layard's explorations, talk about what it would have been like to have been a member of the archaeological team.

- Why do you think God sent Jonah to Ninevah? How did the "revival" at Ninevah impact the nation? What was God's plan for the Assyrian people? (Refer to Isaiah 7:17-20)

- After reading the book of Jonah, look in a Bible handbook or commentary to discover more information. Where is Tarshish located? Where is Ninevah located? How did Jonah get to Ninevah? Why did Jonah get upset when the Ninevites repented? Austen Layard, in his book **Discoveries Among the Ruins of Ninevah**, mentions Jonah's tomb in Ninevah. If Jonah remained after the people repented, what do you think he may have done?

- Not much is known about the daily life of the common people in Assyria, though it appears that their lives were significantly controlled by the "government". However, there is much information about the captives and slaves of Assyrian conquest. What can you discover about this culture in regards to their treatment of other peoples?

- The Assyrians were remarkably adept at capturing fortified cities. What kind of techniques and machinery did they use for this purpose?

- The relief sculptures on the palace walls at Ninevah show the king hunting lions. What might this indicate about the attitude of the rulers?

- Imagine you live inside Jerusalem during the reign of King Hezekiah. What would you think and what would you do when King Sennacherib of Assyria began to lay siege to your city?

Teaching Time!

Seminar Outline

◇ VI. Assyria *— Most powerful kingdom in 760 BC*
  ◇ A) The prophet Jonah (760 B.C.) *—sent to Ninevah*
    Brutal ◇ 1) Tried to go to Tarshish
    ◇ 2) Received a second chance
    ◇ 3) Preached at Ninevah
    ◇ 4) Upset with God when people repented
  ◇ B) Israel taken captive (722 B.C.) *—uses Assyria to bring judgement to Northern Kingdom of Israel*
    ◇ 1) Amos prophesies to Israel
    ◇ 2) Hosea prophesies to Israel
  ◇ C) Judah under siege by Assyria 701 B.C. (2 Kings 19:35)
    ◇ 1) King Hezekiah's response
    ◇ 2) Isaiah's prophecy
    ◇ 3) 185,000 Assyrian soldiers slain by the Lord *—God sends Death Angel to answer Hezekiah's prayer*
    ◇ 4) King Sennacherib assassinated by sons
  ◇ D) The prophet Nahum (660 B.C.)
    ◇ 1) Ninevah to be destroyed by flood (Nahum 1:8)
    ◇ 2) Ninevah's location to be forgotten (Na. 3:11,17, & Zeph. 2:13-15)
  ◇ E) Ninevah destroyed 612 B.C.
    ◇ 1) Tigris River overflowed just as God said!
    ◇ 2) Babylon and Persian armies and destroy city

Walls 100 feet high — Moat 60'x50' — 20 yrs food/water supply

mid 1800's Ninevah discovered

Timeline

→ On your timeline, mark Jonah, Israel's captivity, King Hezekiah, Isaiah, Nahum, King Asshurbanipal, destruction of Ninevah, Layard's discovery of Ninevah.

Research & Reporting:

• Find one of the books listed at the beginning of this unit, along with the encyclopedia or other history resource book for basic information on Assyria/Iraq.

- Investigate the books of Amos and Hosea in the Old Testament. To whom were these prophets speaking? What was the message? How did the people respond? How did God deal with them?

- Do a research paper with pictures on the Assyrians' siege techniques and how effective they were.

- Find out what Assyrians did with the cities they captured. How did this impact the northern kingdom of Israel? (Deportation)

- In Scripture, discover what problem the Assyrians needed to remedy in the northern kingdom after taking the Israelites captive.

- Research and write about how Samaria came to have it's blended religion. Notice how this effects the conversation in John 4.

- Research and explain what cuneiform is, and how it was deciphered in modern times. Explain the significance of the discovery of the library of Asshurbanipal in Ninevah in understanding cuneiform.

- Research and report on the "Rise and Fall of the Assyrian Empire."

- Compile a list of names, dates and accomplishments of Assyria's key leaders. How does this list compare with the events listed in the Bible? (Jonah, captivity of Israel, siege of Judah, destruction of Ninevah)

- In the library or on the Internet, research any information related about the kingdom of Assyria during the Persian Gulf war. (Newspapers, magazines, books, videos) **HINT:** Look for information about Babylon at the same time. (Why?)

- Investigate the history of Iraq from the time of the Assyrians to the present. Report your findings as if you were a newspaper reporter. (Journalism)

- Compare and contrast the history of Iraq and the history of Israel. What cultural distinctives continue throughout the centuries in each nation, i.e. religion, war, politics, class structure?

- Summarize the factors that led to Assyria's far- reaching dominion and the factors leading to their decline.

- On a topographical map, locate Jerusalem. Describe and draw the terrain surrounding Jerusalem, where Sennacherib and his soldiers would have stationed themselves during the siege.

• The Scriptures tell us that 185,000 soldiers were killed in one night by the Angel of the Lord. Would this number have been sufficient to threaten the safety of Jerusalem? (**Hint:** Compare modern battles to determine your answer.)

• Research the life of Isaiah in the Scriptures; the life of King Hezekiah.

• What was the short term result in Judah of God's deliverance from the Assyrians? What was the long term result?

• Look up Sennacherib in your history resources. How significant was this leader in Assyrian history? How was that empire affected by his death?

• Read Nahum 1:8. Though there are a few dissenting opinions, most scholars believe that in 612 B.C. the Tigris River flooded and broke through the city of Ninevah's defenses. The Babylonians and Persians were laying siege to the city, and were in a perfect position to take advantage of this circumstance. Read Matthew 25:52. How does this Scripture portray the inevitability of the fall of Assyria?

• Summarize, either in written or verbal form, what you know about:

   1) the role of Jonah in Assyrian history;
   2) God's timing in sending Jonah;
   3) the effect of Israel's not obeying God, nor receiving His correction;
   4) the effect of Judah's dependence and obedience to God;
   5) the truth of Scriptural prophecies in relation to Assyria's destruction.

Vocabulary

Sargon II	Ninevah	Siege engines
Tiglath-Pileser	Nimrud	Bas-relief
Nimrod	Khorsabad	Lyres
Sennacherib	Mosul	Tribute
Asshurbanipal	Iraq	Cuneiform
Hezekiah	Samaria	Irrigation
Paul Emil Botto	stylus	Deportation
Georg Grotefend		
Austen Layard		

Maps and Mapping

- Using an atlas, encyclopedia or other resource, locate Assyria and the Assyrian Empire on a map.

- What is the name of the country or countries that today occupy the same area as Assyria? What is the capital city, religion, population, major exports, and type of government in each modern country? What is the status of Christian outreach to these countries?

- On a clean worksheet map, draw the boundaries of Assyria (including the conquests), draw the Tigris and Euphrates rivers, label the location of Ninevah and Nimrud. What modern day cities are close to these ancient cities?

- Consult a relief map to discover the terrain of Assyria. Was it desert, mountain, forest, swamp, coastal? What type of climate is typical in that part of the world? How would the terrain and climate have affected the Assyrian culture and God's purpose for it?

Arts in Action

- Try making your own cuneiform book! Items needed: modeling clay, "stylus", knife. Roll clay into flat "slates." Your "stylus" could be a drinking straw cut lengthwise, a wedge-shaped stick, a pencil halved. Make up a simple code, then write a sentence. Show the code to your family. Can anyone read the sentence?

- Draw a picture of a large fish or whale. Now draw a large fish or whale with Jonah inside! Can you draw the fish or whale bones? Is Jonah sitting, kneeling, lying down, standing up? What color is it inside the fish or whale? What color is Jonah?(**Hint:** Many scholars believe that Jonah may have been "bleached" white inside the sea creature, and perhaps that is why the city of Ninevah took his message seriously!) What do Jonah's clothes look like? Does the fish or whale look puzzled?

• Make a soft "stone" relief! Items needed: vermiculite; plaster of Paris; water; bucket; small board for each student; plastic spoon or old tool for carving; aluminum foil; masking tape. Make a "form" for each board with aluminum foil - bring the edges of the foil up 1/2" above the board, secure with masking tape. In a plastic bucket mix 3 scoops vermiculite, 2 scoops plaster of Paris, 2 scoops of water. Stir with a stick until very thick. Pour into aluminum foil form and wait 30 minutes or until hardened. Using plastic spoon, carve a relief sculpture. Possibilities: an animal, a person, a chair, a mountain, a city...   (**Fact:** Much of what is known about the Assyrian civilization was learned from the relief carvings on the walls of the archaeological ruins. Find some photos of these carvings - were the Assyrians very good artists?)

• Make a small "settlement" out of Legos or other building toys. Build a wall around the settlement. Now make a "siege engine" with a battering ram. Add soldiers to the scene. Now reenact either the captivity of Israel or God's deliverance of Judah.

Art Appreciation

• If possible, find these paintings:
 The Defeat of Sennacherib
  by Peter Paul Rubens
 Jonah Cast into the Sea
  by Peter Paul Rubens

Do these paintings reflect what the Bible describes?
How do the paintings differ from your own impression of these historic events?
After observing the paintings, try to draw or paint these same scenes:
  1) imitating Rubens (trace, follow colors, etc.)
  2) creating your own picture

 ## Music

In the archaeological digs of Assyria, many pictures were found of musicians and various types of musical instruments. One can observe different instruments being played at the same time, such as harps and flutes. In fact, one scene from Assyria is that of a king and his queen reclining in their chairs in a lovely garden, while several musicians play (softly?) in the background. Though we do not know what the music sounded like, we can listen to the soothing sounds of the harp and the lilting voice of the flute today.

How do you know which is which? How does the listener know which is the sound of the harp and which is the sound of the flute? If your friend is sitting around the corner, playing a guitar and singing, how do you know that it is a guitar being played rather than a piano or banjo? Or, how can you tell that your friend is singing instead of practicing trumpet?

You might think, "Well, it's obvious! - A trumpet doesn't sound like a voice. And a guitar doesn't sound like a piano or a banjo." That's a very good observation, and what you have just explained is one of the five major elements of music. **Timbre** (sounds like tam-ber) is the name we give this element. Timbre is the uniquely different quality of sound produced by different instruments.

- **Try this:** To experiment with timbre, get your family and friends to gather as many musical instruments as you can find (piano, trumpet, recorder, violin, drum, etc) . Add some non-musical instruments as well, such as metal pots and wooden spoons. While the rest close their eyes, let one person pluck, blow or tap an instrument. Can anyone determine which instrument is being played just by its sound? Let everyone have a turn.

- Now, listen to some recordings of various types of music. Can you identify any of the instruments being played? Listen for percussion, woodwinds, brass and strings. If there are singers, listen for the differences in men's, women's, and children's voices.

Peter and the Wolf by Prokofiev and **A Young Person's Guide to the Orchestra** by Benjamin Britten are musical pieces written to help families become familiar with the different instruments in the symphonic orchestra. These are highly regarded as an introduction to the element of timbre.

Isn't it wonderful that God gave us more than one sound to use in music? Thank you Lord, for giving us different timbres.

 Cooking!

The Assyrians used barley as one of their primary grains. Though this recipe was not found in the ruins (!), it will give you a taste of the foods of this culture.

Barley Soup   Serves 8.

1 1/2 cups barley, soaked overnight in water
2 cups water
1 tsp salt
1 cup onion, chopped fine
4 cups yogurt, plain
2 tbsp fresh coriander (or 1/2 tbsp dried)

1 egg, lightly beaten
3 tbsp butter
1 tbsp. flour
    4 cups chicken broth
    white pepper

Drain barley and place in saucepan with water and salt. Cover tightly and simmer until barley has absorbed all liquid, and grains are separated, about one hour. Add more water only if necessary. Cook onion in butter until soft but not brown. Stir in yogurt. Remove from heat. Mix egg and flour together and blend into the yogurt mixture. Bring the chicken stock to a boil in a large saucepan; stir in yogurt mixture and barley. Add pepper and salt. Pour into bowls and sprinkle with coriander.

Idea Time!

Creative Writing

- Write a fictional account of Jonah's experience hiking across the desert to Ninevah.
- Be a newspaper reporter for the "Assyria Intelligencer" and write an exposé on Sennacherib's defeat at Jerusalem.
- Imagine you are one of those Israelites taken into slavery by King Sargon II. Write a coded message to your cousin in Jerusalem.
- You are with Layard at the discovery of Ninevah. Write a letter "home" to tell your family about the happenings of the dig.
- Finish this limerick about Jonah's "pity party" after God forgave the Ninevites:
    "There was a young man from Israel,
    Who honestly felt rather miserable..."

Art

- As a political cartoonist for the local "Jerusalem News" in 701 B.C., draw your version of the Rabshakeh (messenger from Sennacherib), or of what recently transpired outside the city gates.
- Illustrate a book for young children showing Assyria from the time of Jonah to it's destruction in 612 B.C.

Drama

- Act out the book of Jonah. Use your imagination to create props, sets and costumes. Be sure to include realistic mourning and rejoicing!
- This would be a great time to learn more about **pantomime**. Mime Jonah's being swallowed, being spit out and walking for days across the desert.
- Perform the scene with King Hezekiah, the prophet Isaiah, and the people of J Jerusalem as they are attacked by the Assyrians. Set up the surprise ending!
- Portray Austen Layard's excitement when he discovered Ninevah.
- Do a humorous skit about scoffers in the 1800's being confronted with Layard's discovery.

The Big Picture

- How can you present what you've learned about Assyria and the Bible? How can you demonstrate the faithfulness and justice of God? Share with your family, church, support group, school, or neighbors this exciting look at God's grace in dealing with this nation and also with the Hebrews.

Unit Seven

Babylon and the Captivity of Judah

Judean Captives

Unit Objectives:

- to understand the importance of Babylon in the history of redemption;

- to become familiar with the culture, architecture, and ruins of Babylon;

- to understand the place of the Biblical prophets in the history of Babylon and Judah;

- to examine God's sovereignty and His ways in the history of Babylon, Judah, and the life of King Nebuchadnezzar;

- to apply what is learned about the God's faithfulness as He fulfills His word in our own lives.

Meet the People

- **The Holy Bible**
  Read Genesis 10:8-10; 2 Kings 20-25; 2 Chronicles 32:23-36:21; Psalm 137; Daniel 1-5, 7-8; Habakkuk. Also read Isaiah, Jeremiah, Lamentations, Ezekiel, Zephaniah, Micah.

- **Heroes & Warriors: Nebuchadnezzar** by Mark Healy
  This is a fairly detailed, fairly dry book about King Nebuchadnezzar of Babylon. However, it is the only book that we found about this important historical figure.
  Junior High and up.

- **The Seven Wonders of the Ancient World** by Robert Silverberg
  The Hanging Garden of Babylon was one of the wonders of the ancient world, along with the Pyramid of Cheops (Egypt), the statue of Zeus (Greece), the temple of Artemis (Ephesus), the Mausoleum of Halicarnassus (Asia Minor), the Colossus of Rhodes (Rhodes) and the Pharos Lighthouse (Alexandria, Egypt). This is an excellent introduction containing fascinating stories about these man-made marvels.
  Upper elem and up.

- **Fired Up! - Making Pottery in Ancient Times**
  Pottery is the most basic "book" archaeologist read as they try to understand ancient civilizations. This book is filled with pictures and descriptions of the types of pottery found in archaeological digs. Fascinating!
  Upper elem and up.

- Video: **The Sevens Wonders of the Ancient World** by Questar
  Absolutely captivating! This video really makes these wonders come to life, and helps us to understand more about the geography, the history and the cultures of the seven locations.
  Great for the family!

- Video: **Gateway to the Gods: Babylon** Anthony Roland Collection
  Probably available from a university or state library, this film gives an excellent understanding of the ruins of Babylon, the archaeological treasures, and the history of this city. Not as exciting as the preceding video, this is still an informative, interesting resource on the history of Babylon.
  Great for the family!

- Be sure to look in study Bibles, handbooks, commentaries, etc. for more archaeological information on Babylon.

Talk Together

• Listen to What in the World's Going on Here?, Tape Two. What was the most interesting aspect to you of the events in Babylon which were mentioned? Why? What questions do you have about this time period that you would like to learn more about?
History Journal: Write those questions down, and as you study more material, write the answers to your questions. Write short bios of the interesting people. Illustrate the bios.

• After reading about the climate, terrain and political situation during the time of King Nebuchadnezzar, describe what it would have been like to be one of the captives taken to Babylon.

• Why do you think God called King Nebuchadnezzar "My servant"? What does that tell us about the kind of people God can use for His purposes?

• After reading the book of Daniel, look in a Bible handbook or commentary to discover more information. Where is Babylon located? Where is Jerusalem located in relation to Babylon? How far apart are they?

• What can you discover about this culture in regards to their treatment of other peoples? How do the Babylonians compare to the Assyrians in this regard?

• Talk about Habakkuk 3:16-19. What kind of response did Habakkuk have at the time of the invasion of Jerusalem? What kind of response would you have had? How does this apply to your life right now?
History Journal: Write down the impact of Habakkuk 3:16-19 on your own life.

• Why do you think that God kept showing King Nebuchadnezzar the future? Why do you think God allowed him to see not only the three Hebrew children in the fiery furnace, but the fourth "like the Son of Man" as well? What was King Nebuchadnezzar's eventual response to God?

• Babylon was the most magnificent city of antiquity. Read about the way King Nebuchadnezzar rebuilt the city, the Ishtar Gate, the temples, etc. What do you think it would have been like to be a worshipper of Jehovah living in this city? What about an artist/craftsman? A slave? A soldier?

• When the prophet Jeremiah told the people to settle down in Babylon, build homes and plant vineyards, they knew their time in captivity would not be short (Jer. 29:4-7). Imagine you are a the Jewish mother or father of children born in Babylon. How would you describe what "home" was like? What reasons would you give for the captivity?

• Why do you think that King Belshazzar ordered the vessels of gold from the Temple at Jerusalem to be used for his drunken party? What was the result?

2/19/05

Tape 2 Side 1

Teaching Time!

Seminar Outline

empire lasted 87 tour

◇ VII. Babylon and the Captivity of Judah
◇   A) Judah's Prophets
◇   1) Joel (835 B.C.)
◇   2) Isaiah (740 B.C.)
◇   3) Micah (735 B.C.)   *Before captivity*
◇   4) Zephaniah (630 B.C.)
◇   5) Jeremiah (627 B.C.)
◇   6) Habakkuk (607 B.C.)
◇   B) Judah taken captive by Babylon in 3 stages   King
◇   1) Daniel and others taken 605 B.C.   Nebuchadnezzar
◇   2) Ezekiel and others taken 597 B.C.
◇   3) Jerusalem destroyed 586 B.C.
◇   C) King Nebuchadnezzar - Babylonian King
◇   1) God's perspective
◇   a) Jer. 27:8   Judah would serve King Neb   (623 BC)
◇   b) Jer. 25:9   Neb "my servant"
◇   2) God's involvement   Daniel could interpret dreams
◇   a) dream: Daniel 2:36 - 45   so King Neb relied on him
◇   b) fiery furnace: Daniel 3
◇   c) warning: Daniel 4:19-37
◇   D) Fall of Babylon (539 B.C.)
◇   1) Handwriting on the Wall (Daniel 5:1-31)
◇   2) Prophecy fulfilled concerning the duration of captivity
              3) Mighty Babylon prominent for only 73 years

during party something scared called Daniel to interpret

that very night Belshazzar was killed

a measure a kingdom

Timeline

➔   On your timeline, mark Hammurabi, the prophets of Judah, King
     Nebuchadnezzar, Judah's captivity, King Belshazzar.

descendent of Nebuchadnezzar

drank wine from gublets from Jerusalem

Research & Reporting:

- Find one of the books listed at the beginning of this unit, along with the encyclopedia or other history resource book for basic information on the kingdoms of Babylon, both the early one under Hammurabi and the later under King Nebuchadnezzar.

- Investigate the books of Micah, Zephaniah, and Habakkuk in the Old Testament. To whom were these prophets speaking? What was the message? How did the people respond? How did God deal with them?

- Do a research paper with pictures on the Hanging Garden of Babylon. If you can find the information, include the Walls of Babylon (once included on the list of Wonders of the World!) Discover how the list of the Seven Ancient Wonders of the World was compiled.

- Find out more about King Hammurabi, the code of laws he gave, and his impact on the early city of Babylon.

- Research and report on the "Rise and Fall of the Babylonian Empire."

- In Scripture, discover what was Daniel's role in the government of Babylon.

- Research and write about the three stages of captivity Judah experienced.

- Read about pottery in antiquity, and how it is used in modern times by archaeologists to understand ancient cultures. What are some potential difficulties with this system?

- In the library or on the Internet, research any information related about the kingdom of Babylon (newspapers, magazines, books, videos.) Now compile a list of names, dates and accomplishments of Babylon's key leaders. How does this list compare with the events listed in the Bible?

- Investigate the history of Babylon from the time of Nimrod to the present. Be sure to include Alexander the Great's use of Babylon. Report your findings as if you were a newspaper reporter. (Journalism)

- Examine the "Table of Nations" in Genesis 10. Research and report on these nations and their impact on history. (**Hint:** Josephus relates that at the time of Alexander the Great, most of the names and places were changed to Greek. That is why it is so difficult, though not impossible, to trace them.) How does Acts 17:26 apply to this?

- Babylon is mentioned from Genesis to Revelation. List the verses relating to this city, and chart what the Bible says about Babylon (chronologically.)

- Compare and contrast the history of Babylon (Iraq) and the history of Israel. What cultural distinctives continue throughout the centuries in each nation? (i.e. religion, war, politics, class structure)

- Summarize the factors that led to Babylon's far- reaching dominion, and the factors leading to its decline.

- On a topographical map, locate Babylon. What kind of terrain and ecosystem is there? How did the Babylonians grow food? Research and report on this aspect of Babylon.

- What was the short term result of the captivity in Babylon? What was the long term result?

- Look up King Nebuchadnezzar in your history resources. How significant was this leader in Babylonian history? How was that empire affected by his death? What does Daniel say about the attitude of the king in his last days?

- Research and report on Robert Koldewey, the German archaeologist who excavated Babylon from 1899 - 1913. What did he discover?

- Read about the technique of irrigation in Babylon. How and why do archaeologists believe the Hanging Garden was built? Compare and contrast the difficulty in normal irrigation and the type of irrigation the Hanging Garden would have required.

- Summarize, either in written or verbal form, what you know about:

  1) the disobedience of Judah;
  2) the warnings of the prophets;
  3) the chastisement delivered by Nebuchadnezzar;
  4) the confrontation by God in Nebuchadnezzar's life;
  5) the fall of the Babylonian Empire.

Vocabulary

deportation	irrigation	chastise	scourge
judgment	remnant	Gate of Ishtar	soothsayer
empire	administrator	Daniel	Shadrach
Meshach	Abednego	Hammurabi	Nebuchadnezzar
Belshazzar	Koldewey	pottery	

**Maps
and
Mapping**

- Using an atlas, encyclopedia or other resource, locate Babylon and the Babylonian Empire on a map.

- What is the name of the country or countries that today occupy the same area as the ancient empire? What is the capital city, religion, population, major exports, and type of government in each modern country? What is the status of Christian outreach to these countries?

- On a clean worksheet map, draw the boundaries of Babylon (including the conquests), draw the Tigris and Euphrates rivers, and the cities of the Empire.. What modern day cities are close to these ancient cities?

- Consult a relief map to discover the terrain of Babylon. Was it desert, mountain, forest, swamp, coastal? What type of climate is typical in that part of the world? How would the terrain and climate have affected the Babylonian culture and God's purpose for it?

 Arts in Action

- Try making a miniature version of the Hanging Gardens. You may wish to make it with papier maché, Legos, wood, styrofoam... If it is sturdy enough, line the top with plastic, add sand mixed with dirt, and plant some small flowers. Consult the library or an expert for more information on container gardening! (Check **Teaching History Through Art** for more projects.)

- Draw a picture of Daniel's vision of the four empires. Using the interpretation given by Daniel in Daniel 2, portray the differing aspects of these four empires. Check what you learn about Babylon, Persia, Greece and Rome with the Biblical description.

• Make a "wall" of bricks to paint: On a piece of wood, roll out clay, or bread dough, or plaster, etc.. Mark lines in it while still soft to resemble bricks. After the wall dries, paint the wall blue using either tempera or acrylic to cover completely. After this layer dries, paint designs on selected bricks with bright colors. If you painted fierce animals, as the Babylonians did, would you be frightened to walk by this wall?

Art Appreciation

• If possible, find this painting:
  Belshazzar's Feast
  by Rembrandt

  Does this painting reflect what the Bible describes?
  How does it differ from your own impression of these historic events?
  After observing the paintings, try to draw or paint these same scenes:
  1) imitating Rembrandt (trace, follow colors, etc.)
  2) creating your own picture

• Also, look for artists' depiction of the Hanging Garden of Babylon.
  Do they seem realistic? Impressive? Beautiful?

 ## Music

Daniel 3:5-30 is the story about the three Hebrews thrown into the fiery furnace for not bowing down to worship a golden image. What was the signal that everyone should bow down? The playing of horns, flutes, harps, lyres and psalteries (probably a form of dulcimer). These instruments were played at the same time, creating a **symphonic** sound.

• Listen to a recording of a solo instrument (guitar, piano, etc.) Now, listen to a recording of a symphony (i.e. by Haydn or Brahms.) Notice the difference in sound between an ensemble of instruments and a solo instrument. In a previous unit we talked about the unique timbre of each instrument, but now listen to the wonderful sounds created when different kinds of instruments are played together. Instruments that have the same basic characteristics are said to be in a family of instruments. In other words, violin, cello, and harp are in the string family; trumpet, trombone, french horn are in the brass family; clarinet, flute, saxophone are in the woodwind family; and drums, cymbals, rhythm instruments are in the percussion family.

• **Field Trip:** Perhaps there is a church, school or philharmonic in your area with an orchestra or band performing a concert you can attend. Listen for the sounds of the different families of instruments and how they blend together to make the music.

Science

• Contact the local County Extension office to learn about gardening in different kinds of soil, different climates, and irrigation. Then plant at least two different mini-gardens in containers. One should be for plants which thrive in hot, dry climates, another should be for moisture-loving, shade plants. What kind of obstacles would the architect of the Hanging Gardens of Babylon have had to overcome?

• One resource on the Hanging Gardens said that the rooms under the garden area were kept cool in the summer by the foliage of the plants and by the evaporating water. Discover what "swamp coolers" are, and how they function. Experiment with the cooling process of evaporation: 1) on a hot day, put room temperature water on your face and arms. As it evaporates, does it cool? 2) on a hot day, find some leafy trees or an arbor to sit under. Is it cooler among the leaves? Devise your own experiments.

Cooking

Those who were taken captive by Babylon had many changes to adjust to, including unusual and unfamiliar ingredients for basic food. It was undoubtedly a difficult time, but the routine of daily life had its own comforts. Try this unusual "comfort food" and rejoice in the goodness and dependability of the Lord!

Ezekiel's Many-Floured Bread

2 tbsp yeast
1 1/2 cup warm water
1 egg
1/4 cup oil (plus 1 tbsp to brush top of bread)
1/3 cup honey
2 1/2 tsp salt
1 tbsp. cumin

1 tbsp. coriander seed
1/ 4 cup lentil flour
1/4 cup barley flour
1/4 cup fava (broad bean) flour
1/4 cup millet flour
2 cups whole wheat flour
2 - 2 1/2 cups unbleached flour

Dissolve yeast in warm water. Mix in next 5 ingredients. Stir in all flours, except white flour, and beat well. Add enough white flour to make a dough that can be gathered into a ball. Turn onto lightly floured surface and knead 10 minutes. Place in greased bowl, turning over to grease surface. Cover with a cloth and let rise in warm place until double in bulk, about 1 1/2 hours. Punch down and let rise again about 1 hour. Shape into 2 round loaves and place on greased baking sheet. Cover and let rise 1 hour. Bake in 350 oven for about 30 minutes. Remove, brush with remaining oil. Makes 2 loaves.

Idea Time!

Creative Writing

- Write a short story from the perspective of Daniel's mother in Jerusalem.

- Retell the captivity of Judah using modern names and terms.

- Be a newspaper reporter for the "The Babylon Babbler" and write the fast-breaking stories of "Three Engage in Civil Disobedience, Come Out Smelling Like a Rose?" and "Fourth Figure Found in Fire!"

- Discover the connection these words have to the unit, and then write a rhyming poem using them:
    irrigation, evaporation, deportation   *(Babylon)*
    demonstrate, illustrate, appreciate   *(Daniel)*
    weep, reap, leap   *(Judah)*

Art

- As a political cartoonist, do a series of cartoons about King Nebuchadnezzar's confrontations with God's power.

Drama

- Act out the incident of the handwriting on the wall. Use your imagination to create props, sets and costumes. Be sure to include realistic fear!

- Do a humorous skit about Nebuchadnezzar, his pride, going crazy, and his eventual repentance.

- Put on a puppet show showing the young men with Daniel who refused the king's rich food. Be sure to show the effects of the rich diet on other young men!

The Big Picture

- How can you present what you've learned about the Babylonian Empire and the Bible? Come up with a plan to share with your family, church, support group, school, or neighbors this exciting look at God's grace and justice in dealing with this nation, and also with the Hebrews.

Unit Eight

The Persians and Medes

Mordecai honored by Haman

Unit Objectives:

- to understand the fulfillment of prophecy and God's faithfulness in the rebuilding of the Temple in Jerusalem;

- to compare and contrast the previous empires and the Medo-Persian Empire;

- to comprehend the significance of Daniel's vision in relation to the Medo-Persian Empire and the struggle with Greece;

- to understand the book of Esther and the feast of Purim in light of this historical empire;

- to gain a thorough understanding of the geography of the Middle East, Asia Minor and Greece.

Meet the People

- **The Holy Bible**
  Read 2 Chronicles 36:22-23; Isaiah 13:17-19, 44:24-28, 45:1-7; Daniel 2:39, 5:30-31, 6:1-28, 9:1-11:2; Ezra, Esther, Nehemiah, Haggai, Zechariah, Malachi.

- **World Leaders Past and Present: Xerxes** by Morgan Llwelyn
  Written in a very interesting style, this is an excellent book about a fascinating leader! This is a must-read for older students as it will give a very thorough understanding of the most significant king of Persia. **Junior High and up.**

- **Behold Your Queen!** by Gladys Malvern
  Historical fiction concerning Esther, this wonderful book makes the details of the book of Esther come to life. My only complaint was that it did not tell the reader that King Ahasuerus was another name for King Xerxes. **Upper elem and up.**

- **Stories from Herodotus** translated by Glanville Downey
  Absolutely a must! This book is a children's version of the ancient Greek historian, Herodotus, and it details the invasion of Greece by the Persians in 490 B.C. and 480 B.C. We couldn't put it down. **Upper elem and up.**

- **The Lion in The Gateway** by Mary Renault
  A fictional account for children of the Persian invasion of Greece. The battles of Marathon, Thermopylae, and Salamis are described in rich detail. You will not understand the history of Persia or Greece without understanding these battles.
  Upper elem and up.

- **Children of the Fox** by Jill Paton Walsh
  This book could be read either in this unit or the unit on Greece. It also fictionalizes the Persian invasion (led by Xerxes) of Greece in 480 B.C. Written as three short stories about Greek children, it includes a story about the aftermath of the invasion which helps one understand the reason for the Peloponnesian wars between Athens and Sparta. **Great for the family!**

- **Exploits of Xenophon** translated by Geoffrey Household
  This is an incredible, riveting book! It is the true, autobiographical account of Greek mercenaries fighting for a Persian governor who wishes to usurp the throne and become king. **Great read aloud!**

Talk Together

- Listen to What in the World's Going on Here?, Tape Two. What was the most interesting aspect to you of the events in the Medo-Persian Empire which were mentioned? Why? What questions do you have about this time period that you would like to learn more about?

    History Journal: Write those questions down, and as you study more material, write the answers to your questions. Write short bios of the interesting people. Illustrate the bios.

- Why do you think God called King Cyrus by name in Isaiah 44 - 45? When was the book of Isaiah written? When did King Cyrus appear on the scene of history? Why would God direct Isaiah to prophecy about a non-Jewish king?

- What can you discover about this culture in regards to their treatment of other people? How does it differ from the treatment of the Assyrians? ... From the Babylonians?

- After reading the book of Esther, look in a Bible handbook or commentary to discover more information. Where is Shushan (Susa) located? Where is Babylon located? Where is Jerusalem located? Are these cities close to one another? How far did the Jews have to go to return to Jerusalem? How far did Mordecai and Esther have to travel from Babylon to Shushan?

- Read one of the books about Xerxes' invasion of Greece. Imagine you are one foot soldier among hundreds of thousands. When you are told to cross the bridge over the Hellespont, what is your reaction? Describe the bridge, how it was made, and what it felt like to cross it.

- Do you think Xerxes planned his invasion well? Why or why not? Do you think he had any concept of what would happen at Thermopylae or the Battle of the Bay of Salamis? What do you think he should have done differently?

- Read Ezra 8:21-23. Imagine you are one of the people returning to Jerusalem with Ezra. Describe the thoughts and feeling of the people as they fast and pray to God, rather than requesting military escorts from the king. Was it dangerous to travel that far in those days? When has your family chosen to trust God in prayer, rather than rely on human wisdom?

- Nehemiah describes building the wall of Jerusalem. Why are city walls so important? What role did Nehemiah play in the rebuilding of the wall? How did the laborers work on the wall?

- Why do you think that not all of the Jews returned to Jerusalem? What was it like in Jerusalem before the rebuilding took place? What was it like in Babylon? What was it like under Persian rule?

- Imagine you are Esther. Describe why it is so scary to go to the king.

Tape 2 side 1

Teaching Time!

Seminar Outline

◇ VIII. Medo-Persian Empire, the second empire of Daniel's vision
◇   A) Cyrus the Great of Persia
◇   1) Isaiah's Prophecies:
◇   *740BC* a) Isaiah 44:28,
◇   b) Isaiah 45:l (written c. 700 B.C.)
◇   2) His accomplishments
◇   *536 BC* a) 2 Chronicles 36:22-23 *- commanded to build Temple in Jerusalem*
◇   b) Ezra 1 - 3
◇   B) Jews return to Jerusalem
◇   *last 3 Books about history of Jews* 1) Zerubbabel rebuilds the temple - Ezra 1-6
◇   2) Ezra returns - Ezra 7-l0
◇   3) Nehemiah rebuilds the wall - Nehemiah
◇   4) Prophets
◇   a) Haggai
◇   b) Zechariah
◇   c) Malachi - 425 B.C. (last prophetic word before Messiah)
◇   C) Persians & Medes fight the Greeks
◇   1) King Darius
◇   a) Battle of Marathon
◇   2) Xerxes
◇   a) Invasion of Greece 480 B.C.
◇   b) Book of Esther

Babylon fell 539 BC

Timeline

→ On your timeline, mark Cyrus' proclamation, return of Jews, Temple rebuilt, battle of Marathon, Xerxes, battle of Bay of Salamis, Esther, Nehemiah, Malachi.

Research & Reporting:

- Find one of the books listed at the beginning of this unit, along with the encyclopedia or other history resource book for basic information on the Persian invasions of Greece. What was the short term impact of these invasions upon the Medo-Persian Empire? What was the long term impact upon Greece?

- Investigate the books of Haggai, Zechariah, and Malachi in the Old Testament. To whom were these prophets speaking? What was the message? How did the people respond? How did God deal with them?

- Do a research paper with pictures on the Royal Road of Persia between Sardis and Susa. To what short-lived American endeavor can it be likened?

- Discover the method used in creating Xerxes' floating bridge which spanned the Hellespont. What materials were used? How was it constructed? How stable would it have been? How many troops crossed it? What else crossed it? How long did it take? Was the bridge there when the army returned from Greece? **For Extra Credit:** Learn more about modern floating bridges. The Department of Transportation in Washington state has some wonderful information, including videos, about their floating bridges. Contact:
  Mr. Brent Olsen
  WSDOT
  P O Box 330310, MS 103
  Seattle, WA 98135-9710
  On the Internet: http:// www.wsdot.wa.gov

- Research and write about the Feast of Purim, both the historical beginnings and the modern day celebration.

- Research and report on the "Rise and Fall of the Medo-Persian Empire." Who finally conquered this empire?

- Compile a list of names, dates and accomplishments of Media's and Persia's key leaders . How does this list compare with the events listed in the Bible?

- Investigate, using the library or the Internet, the history of Persia and Media from the time of King Cyrus to the present. What is the modern name of this nation? You may wish to interview adults who remember the deposing of the Shah. Report your findings as if you were a newspaper reporter. (Journalism)

- Look up Xerxes in your history resources. How significant was this leader in Medo-Persian history? How was that empire affected by his death?

- Research and report on the rebuilding of the Temple and the wall of Jerusalem. Make a chart showing both the history of the Temple from the time of Solomon until the present and the history of Jerusalem from David to the present.

• Research and report on the immense army of Xerxes. Where did his soldiers come from? Describe Xerxes special fighting unit. How was Xerxes' army reprovisioned as they traveled? How many returned?

• Discover the tactics of the Greeks in fighting the Battle of the Bay of Salamis. Where did Xerxes' ships come from? How did he get them to Greece? (**Hint:** Find out about the canal.) How did Xerxes' navy lose the battle? Describe the differences between the Medo-Persian ships and the Greek ships. (See Unit Ten for more resources.)

• After reading about the Greek victories over the Medes and Persians, research the history of Western civilization. Make a simple chart showing the flow of Western civilization from the time of the Greeks to the present. Make a chart showing the flow of history in the Middle East from the time of the Medes and Persians. Show the differences between the two, and explain what the impact of a Medo-Persian victory at Salamis would have had upon history.

• Summarize, either in written or verbal form, what you know about:

> 1) King Cyrus;
> 2) King Xerxes;
> 3) The invasions of Greece;
> 4) Esther;
> 5) Jews returning to Jerusalem;
> 6) Rebuilding the Temple;
> 7) Rebuilding the Wall;
> 8) Obedience to the Commandments.

Vocabulary

repatriate	invasion	trireme
Bay of Salamis	Hellespont	tactics
Purim	Media	Persia
Royal Road	Thermopylae	Marathon
Athens	Persepolis	Susa
Cyrus	Darius	Xerxes
Artaxerxes		
Law of the Persians and Medes		

Hands On!

**Maps
and
Mapping**

- Using an atlas, encyclopedia or other resource, locate ancient Persia and Media on a map.

- What is the name of the country or countries that today occupy the same area as the Medo-Persian Empire? What is the capital city, religion, population, major exports, and type of government in each modern country? What is the status of Christian outreach to these countries?

- On a clean worksheet map, draw the boundaries of Persia/Media (including the conquests), draw the Tigris and Euphrates rivers, the Persian Gulf, label the location of Persepolis and Susa. What modern day cities are close to these ancient cities?

- Consult a relief map to discover the terrain of Persia and Media. Was it desert, mountain, forest, swamp, coastal? What type of climate is typical in that part of the world? How would the terrain and climate have affected the Medo-Persian culture and God's purpose for it?

 Arts in Action

- Try making a relief carving on wax or soap. (See Resource List for soap-making kit.) Or, with a slab of clay rolled flat onto a board, carve a relief of a simple animal, such as a fish. Let it dry and mount it.

- A wonderful bronze head (cast, not sculptured) was found in the excavations of Persia. Make a sand cast candle (pour hot wax into a form made in the sand), or, if you are very adventurous, try making a plaster cast. Check the library or an expert for more info.

- In the Book of Esther, the king gives to Haman and then to Mordecai his signet ring. A signet ring was extremely important because it was stamped on official documents (much like a signature today). Create a stamp using a potato! Check the library or an expert for information about potato printing.

- Build a "floating bridge" out of Legos or other materials. Anchor ships across the span. Make miniature cables and string them across the tops of the ships. Add planking, railing, etc.

Art Appreciation

- Find pictures of the ruins of Persepolis (check the encyclopedia). Also look for cylinder seals which show the art of Persia and Media.

What can you learn about this culture from its art?
Did the Persians and Medes create any art that was unique, or was it all borrowed from previous civilizations?
What is the outstanding feature of Medo-Persian art?

 ## Music

After the plot of Haman was uncovered, the Jews were allowed to defend themselves on the day of attack. Their defense was so successful that the Jewish nation survived this effort to annihilate them. In response, the people celebrated with feasting and joy. Though the Bible does not describe the music of the celebration, we know that the Jews had used music in celebrations in the past.

Do you think the music would have been loud or soft? Or, perhaps would it have been a combination of loud and soft? The term used to describe the loudness or softness in music is **dynamics**. Dynamics is another one of the fundamental elements of music. A piece of music can be played all at a loud dynamic level, or it can be played at a soft dynamic level, but most music has a combination of various dynamic levels.

A wonderful example of strong dynamic changes is the "Surprise Symphony" by Franz Joseph Haydn. He wrote strong contrasts of dynamics in this piece of music to address a problem. He was a diligent, hardworking, Christian composer who greatly respected the musicians in his orchestra. However, the rich people who came to hear the orchestra often fell asleep due to too much feasting and drinking. So he devised a solution! Listen carefully to the second movement called the "Andante" to hear what this solution was. Do you think it would have been effective?

- **Try this:** See how softly you can sing or tap or hum; then see how loudly you can sing or tap or hum; then determine how many different levels you can make. For instance, can you sing very, very soft? very soft? soft? medium soft? medium loud? loud? very loud? very, very loud? Musicians use Italian terms to indicate dynamic levels. "Piano" means soft, "forte" (for`-tay) means loud.

Science

The cables used in supporting Xerxes' bridge across the Hellespont were made of flax and papyrus that were braided together. The first bridge attempted also used cables of flax and papyrus, but they were not braided together, and the bridge came apart in a storm.

- Experiment with braiding various short ropes each made with only one substance (thread, string, horse hair, human hair, etc.) Test their strength by hanging weights from the end until the ropes break. Now try braiding different substances together and hanging weights from the rope. Which ropes are the strongest? Does it improve the strength of a rope to use more than one material? **Variation:** Try making a rope that is not braided, and one that is. Which is stronger? Eccl. 4:12

Cooking

Our unit examines both the Medo-Persian Empire, the return of the Jews to Jerusalem, and the deliverance of the Jews recorded in the Book of Esther. When you learn about the climate of Persia, perhaps this soup will sound *just right!* (It is served cold.) And to help you celebrate Purim, we have included a delicious cookie - Rejoice!

Persian Cucumber & Yogurt Soup

1 quart yogurt (plain)   3 small cucumbers, peeled, seeded, chopped
1 cup buttermilk   1/2 cup walnuts, chopped
1/2 cup fresh mint, finely chopped (or chopped green onions)
Beat yogurt and buttermilk together until well blended. Stir in mint and cucumbers; salt and pepper to taste. Serve very cold, sprinkle with chopped walnuts. Serves 8.

Hamantaschen Cookie Recipe (Purim)

1 cup whole wheat flour   1/4 cup butter, softened
1 cup white flour   2 eggs, slightly beaten
2 tsp. baking powder   1 tsp. almond extract
1/2 cup sugar   1/4 cup orange juice
Traditional filling: poppy seed, prune. However, you can also use your imagination and come up with a sure-to-please-the-family filling.
Combine and mix all dry ingredients. Cut in the butter. Add the eggs, almond extract, and juice. Mix dough into a ball, adding extra flour or water if needed for a workable dough. Roll out dough on a floured surface, 1/4" thick. Cut with cookie cutter in 3" circles. Place 1 tsp. filling in the center, and pinch dough up on three sides to form an open triangle. Bake at 350 degrees for 20 min., or until golden.

Idea Time!

Creative Writing

- Write a fictional account of the journey from Babylon to Jerusalem, from the viewpoint of a sheep named "Baa-aa-aa-Hum-bug."
- Be a war correspondent accompanying Xerxes' invasion army. Write a series of news reports for the "Susa Sun" about the invasion of Greece.
- Write a poem that is titled "From Babylon went good Zerubbabel."
- Finish this limerick about Esther's uncle:
    There once was an uncle named Mordecai
    Whose enemies wanted to hang him high...

Art

- Illustrate a book for young children showing the events of Esther's life. Include her someday-to-be husband going off to subdue those rebellious Greeks.

Drama

- Act out the rebuilding of Jerusalem's wall. Begin with Nehemiah's conversation with King Artaxerxes. Use your imagination to create props, sets and costumes. Be sure to include realistic fear and rejoicing!
- Do a dramatic narrative about the invasion of Greece by King Xerxes.
- Create a humorous skit about Haman having to honor Mordecai.
- Portray Esther's invitation to the king and Haman, and the banquets that followed.

The Big Picture

- Plan to celebrate the Feast of Purim. Learn about the traditions and rituals of this feast, prepare costumes and props to tell the story of Esther, and invite your family, friends, or neighbors to share this miraculous event.

- Within the time of celebration, be sure to share what you have learned about the Medo-Persian Empire and how God used it to bring about His purposes. Remember to explain this empire's place in Daniel's vision, as well as what came before and what will come after. Praise the Lord together for His perfect timing, perfect provision and perfect plans!

Unit Nine

Greece

The Parthenon

Unit Objectives:

- to become familiar with the Golden Age of Greece, the Peloponnesian Wars, and Alexander the Great's conquests;

- to learn about the Greek development of science, medicine, math, art, music and architecture;

- to understand the prophetic description of Alexander's empire in the book of Daniel;

- to comprehend the significant impact ancient Greece had upon the world, and to see God's purposes fulfilled;

- to know the worldview of the ancient Greeks, and evaluate its continuing influence in the world today.

Meet the People

• **The Holy Bible**
Read Daniel 7:6; 8:5-8, 21; 11:1-4. Also, read Paul's Mars Hill Sermon in Acts 17.

• **Growing Up in Ancient Greece** by Chris Chelepi
Great overview! This series really helps explain many different aspects of life in ancient times.
Elementary and up.

• **Focus on Ancient Greeks** by Anita Ganeri Published by Aladdin Books
If you can find it, this book is an excellent, multi-faceted look at Greece.
Elementary and up.

• **Famous Men of Greece** edited by Rob Shearer
An excellent, brief introduction to the important historical figures of Greece, written in
biographical style. **Elementary and up.**

• **World Leaders Past and Present: Pericles** by Terry Scott King
This was the Greek leader who masterminded the Golden Age of Greece after the victory over
Xerxes. This series of books is absolutely fantastic reading! **Junior High and up.**

• **In Search of Troy** by Ventura and Ceserani
Piero Ventura is a masterful artist, and his books are always worth searching for. This is the
intriguing story of Heinrich Schliemann, the amateur who discovered Troy. (Probably, the war
between Troy and Greece took place during the time of the Mycenaeans.)
Upper elem and up.

• **Golden Days of Greece** by Olivia Coolidge
This is one of the best authors of short biographies that I've found. Her books are uniformly
interesting and filled with the kinds of tidbits that make history memorable.
Upper elem and up.

• **Herodotus** by Henry Cary
This Greek historian was the first world traveler who kept track of the places he visited.
Herodotus is one of the most important writers of antiquity, and his writings are still
fascinating. **High school and up.**

• **The Greek Hoplite** by Martin Windron
An excellent look at the Greek soldiers, who were among the best fighters of history.
Upper elem and up.

• **Science in Ancient Greece** by Kathlyn Gay
If you skip the second chapter on evolution, the remainder of the book is wonderful! Learn
about many different areas of science which were "pioneered" by the Greeks.
Upper elem and up.

• **Greek Food and Drink** by Irene Tavlarios
One of the best Greek cookbooks I've seen, this delightful book also describes some of the
history of Greek cooking, lots of delectable pictures of food, and more. **Upper elem and up.**

• **Mathematicians are People, Too** by Reimer & Reimer
Three of the earliest named mathematicians in history were Greek. This fascinating book tells the story of these men as well as mathematicians from later times. **Elementary and up.**

• **World Leaders Past and Present: Alexander the Great** by Dennis Wepman
One of the most significant military leaders in world history, Alexander the Great was also a fascinating historical figure. **Junior High and up.**

• **Military History of the World - Volume One** by J.F.C. Fuller
For those who really want to dig into this subject, this is the book to get. It includes some fascinating accounts of Alexander the Great. **High school and up.**

Talk Together

• Listen to What in the World's Going on Here?, Tape Two. What was the most interesting aspect to you of the events in Greece which were mentioned? Why? What questions do you have about this time period that you would like to learn more about?
  History Journal: Write those questions down, and as you study more material, write the answers to your questions. Write short bios of the interesting people. Illustrate the bios.

• After reading about the climate, terrain, and history of Greece (up through Xerxes' failed invasion), what factors do you think contributed to the Greeks' independent way of life?

• Josephus, the ancient Jewish historian, gives a fascinating account of Alexander's time in Jerusalem. Though it is not Scripture, and may not be true, it does give an interesting insight into God's purposes.

"Now Alexander, when he had taken Gaza, made haste to go up to Jerusalem; and Jaddua the high priest, when he heard that, was in an agony, and under terror, as not knowing how he should meet the Macedonians, since the king was displeased at his foregoing disobedience. He therefore ordained that the people should make supplications, and should join with him in offering sacrifice to God, whom he besought to protect that nation, and to deliver them from the perils that were coming upon them; whereupon God warned him in a dream, which came upon him after he had offered sacrifice, that "he should take courage, and adorn the city, and open the gates; that the rest should appear in white garments, but that he and the priests should meet the king in the habits proper to their order, without the dread of any ill consequences, which the providence of God would prevent." Upon which, when he rose from his sleep, he greatly rejoiced; and declared to all the warning he had received from God... The Jews also did altogether, with one voice, salute Alexander, and encompass him about; whereupon the king of Syria, and the rest, were surprised at what Alexander had done, and supposed him disordered in his mind. However, Parmenio alone went up to him, and asked him, "How it came to pass, that when all others adored him, he should adore the high priest of the Jews?" To whom he replied, "I did not adore him, but that God who hath honored him with the high priesthood; for I saw this very person in a dream, in this very habit, when I was at Dios in Macedonia, who, when I was considering with myself how I might obtain the dominion of Asia, exhorted me to make no delay, but boldly to pass over the sea thither, for that he would conduct my army, and would give me the dominion over the Persians..."

- Why do you think God gave Daniel such a clear vision of a Greek king who would quickly sweep through the world, and then be gone just as quickly?

- After reading the eighth and eleventh chapter of Daniel, look in a Bible handbook or commentary to discover more information. How were the prophecies fulfilled?

- What can you discover about the Greek culture in regards to their treatment of other peoples? What purpose did the slaves fulfill? How did that impact the culture and lifestyle of the Greeks?

- Why do you think Greece had its' "Golden Age" after Xerxes' defeat?

- Imagine you were an Athenian. How would you describe Sparta to a foreigner?

- Why do you think the Greek soldiers were so effective? What application of this can you make in your own life? (Ephesians 6:10-17)

- The Greek philosopher and teacher, Aristotle, was Alexander the Great's tutor, prior to his conquests. What kind of impact do you think this famous Greek thinker had upon a Macedonian prince? Explain how this might have made a difference in the long term results of Alexander's conquests.

- Who was Hippocrates? What was his contribution to medical care?

- We will not focus upon the religion of the Greeks. It is, however, important to consider that the gods and goddesses of the Greeks did not act significantly different from sinful man, and were only "greater" in that they were immortal and had magical powers. Read Paul's sermon in Acts 17, and talk about the contrast between God and the Greek gods. (**Recommendation:** For those wishing to pursue this subject from a Christian worldview, we recommend David Quine's **Worldviews of History**.)

- Paul addresses the issue of art in Acts 17:29. What did he say about the Greek purpose in their religious art? Read about the statue of Zeus, built about 430 B.C. Imagine you were an Athenian, that you had seen the statue of Zeus, and you were listening to Paul. How would Paul's words effect you? What response would you give Paul?

- How many more of the seven ancient wonders of the world were "religious art"? How many of these were made by Greeks, or under the influence of the Greeks? Discuss this in light of Acts 17:29. (**Important:** Did Paul try to destroy the statues? Did he walk away in disgust? What did he do? What can we learn from him?)

- Paul, in Acts 17, built a bridge of communication to the Greeks, using familiar things from their culture (statues, poetry, etc.)Talk together as a family about what our response should be to people who are outside of the Christian worldview.

Tape 2 Side 1

Teaching Time!

Seminar Outline

◇ IX. Greece
◇   A) 508 B.C. Athens became a democracy
◇   B) Persia conquered the Greek city states around 500B.C.
◇   C) Revolt by Greeks for 5 years

Greeks won battle of marathon → 26 mi

◇   1) King Darius crushes revolt, sends army to Athens in (490 B.C.)
◇   2) King Xerxes' massive invasion of Greece in 480 B.C.
◇   D) Golden Age *(Persian)*   *→ 2,000,000 soldiers Lost   Ester became 2nd wife*
◇   1) Rebuild Athens
◇   2) Socrates, Plato, Aristotle - Philosophers
◇   3) Art, architecture, theater
◇   E) Peloponnesian Wars - (431 B.C.) - 404 B.C. (Sparta beats Athens)
◇   F) Conquering Empire [SPARTA]   *(city/state)*

Tape 2 Side 2

◇   1) Philip II of Macedonia - 353B.C.
◇   a) Father of Alexander *(tutored by Aristotle)*
◇   b) Murdered in 336 B.C. *— by household servant*
◇   2) Alexander the Great (comes to throne in 336 B.C.)

consolidated Greek States

◇   a) Daniel 11:2-4
◇   b) Daniel 8:21,22   *} Jews allowed to worship as they pleased*
◇   c) Conquering hero in Egypt (filled up the war chest)

was feared

◇   d) Defeats Persia 331 B.C.
◇   e) Conquers northwestern India -325 B.C.
◇   f) Dies in Babylon 323 B.C. (33 years old at death)

Timeline

→ On your timeline, mark the Golden Age of Greece, Socrates, Plato, Aristotle, Pericles, Peloponnesian wars, and Alexander the Great's conquests.

Jeffrey Householder

Research & Reporting:

- Find one of the books listed at the beginning of this unit, along with the encyclopedia or other history resource book for basic information on Greece.

- Do a research paper with diagrams showing Alexander the Great's conquests. Where did he start? Where did he go before Persia? Where did his armies stop? What were his provisioning needs? What were the attitudes of his soldiers and his officers to him?

- Find out who the Peloponnesian war involved, what issues were at stake, and the results (both short term and long term.)

- Use a Bible Concordance (such as Strong's) to discover what the Scripture says about the Greeks. What are the characteristics described? Compare and contrast the Greeks and Jews as described in Scripture.

- Research and write about how science and mathematics were explored by the Greeks. What branches of science did the Greeks develop? What mathematical properties and concepts were discovered by the Greeks?

- Research and explain who Pythagoras was, and his impact upon mathematics and music.

- Research and report on the "Rise and Fall of Alexander's Empire."

- Compile a list of names, dates and accomplishments of Greece's key leaders . Include Themistocles and Xenophon, though they were studied in Persia.

- In the library or on the Internet, research any information related about Greece. (Look at newspapers, magazines, books, videos, etc.) Write to the Greek Embassy to request information about the history, terrain, climate, agriculture, etc., of Greece. Report your findings as if you were a newspaper reporter.

- Discover the beginnings of medical practice. Report your findings.

- On a topographical map, locate Athens, Corinth, Sparta, Mt. Olympus, Ephesus, Halicarnassus, Rhodes, Sardis, Crete. What was the impact of the Mediterranean Sea on the Greek civilization?

- Research Alexander's conquest of Tyre. Read Zech. 9:1-4 and explain how this prophecy, written 150 years earlier, was fulfilled.

- Research and report on the development of the Scientific Method in Greece.

Vocabulary

democracy	sculpture	acropolis	conquest
barbarian	mathematics	spartan	philosopher
debate	Hippocratic Oath	Parthenon	Scientific Method
Aristotle	Thales	Pericles	Xenophon
architecture	column	capital	pedestal

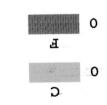
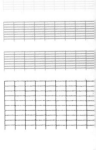

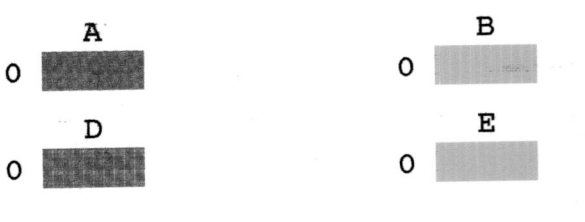

A   B

0   0

D   E

0   0

Hands On!

**Maps
and
Mapping**

- Using an atlas, encyclopedia or other resource, locate Greece on a map.

- What is the name of the country or countries that today occupy the same area as Alexander's empire? What is the capital city, religion, population, major exports, and type of government in each modern country? What is the status of Christian outreach to these countries?

- On a clean worksheet map, draw the boundaries of Greece (also, the conquests of Alexander), label the Mediterranean, the location of Sparta, Athens, Corinth, Bay of Salamis, Macedonia, Ephesus, Crete, Rhodes. What modern day cities are close to these ancient places?

- Consult a relief map to discover the terrain of Greece. Was it desert, mountain, forest, swamp, coastal? What type of climate is typical in that part of the world? How would the terrain and climate have affected the Greek culture and God's purpose for it?

Arts in Action

- Try making a papier maché vase (or tall bowl.) Paint a solid color, then when it is dry, paint your family on the vase. The only portraits done by Greeks were on vases!

- Using modeling clay, try sculpting a head (or an animal.) Check in the library or with an expert for more info. How is this different from the casting process?

- Draw examples of the different Greek columns: Ionic, Dorian and Corinthian.

- "Chisel" a sculpture made of soft stone: 3 scoops vermiculite, 2 scoops plaster of Paris, 2 scoops water. Stir in bucket until it is very thick. Pour into small carton to harden for 30 minutes. Peel off carton and "chisel" with a plastic spoon or knife.

- Using Legos, papier maché, clay or other medium, build a miniature version of Tyre. Demonstrate Alexander's successful techniques for capturing this heretofore unconquered city.

Art Appreciation

- Look at pictures of the Parthenon, of the different styles of Greek columns used in buildings, Greek sculpture, and artists' renditions of the Greek wonders of the world.

What are examples you have seen of art forms borrowed from ancient Greece?

 ## Music

Pythagoras, a Greek mathematician, was walking down the street one day when he heard the sound of four hammers beating on metal. Realizing that the sounds were pleasing to the ear, he recognized the golden opportunity to determine what made them so. The littlest hammer rang out with a higher sound than the others, while the biggest hammer produced the lowest sound. Pythagoras was hearing the "pitch" of the hammers.

Pitch is the musical term used to describe the highness or lowness of sound. It is one of the five elements of music. Sing the first line of "Twinkle, Twinkle Little Star." Which word do you say when you are singing the highest sound? Which word do you say when you are singing the lowest sound? The highest sound is the highest pitch, and the lowest sound is the lowest pitch.

- **Try this:** Using a keyboard or other instrument, have someone play two different notes. With your eyes closed, tell whether the second note is higher or lower than the first. (Thumbs up if the second note is higher, thumbs down if it is lower.) Have each member of the family try this experiment.
  Variation: Play three notes. Determine which one is the highest, which one is the lowest.) How did you do? This is an excellent starting place for learning to distinguish pitch, and for developing a "musical ear."

*When we combine different pitches, the sound can be pleasing (**consonance**) or harsh sounding (**dissonance**). What Pythagoras heard was a pleasing sound (consonance) and he determined to research why these particular hammers sounded good together. What he found was that the hammer with the highest pitch was exactly one-half the size of the hammer with the lowest pitch. The other two hammers also had precise mathematical ratios with the lowest. Pythagoras came up with an explanation of which combinations of notes are consonant and which combinations are dissonant. But the amazing thing about Pythagoras was that he figured it out using mathematical ratios!*

- **Try this:** Sing together "Row, Row, Row Your Boat."
  Now, try singing it as a round with each new part entering when the previous part says: "... your boat." Listen to the sound. Can you hear the different pitches being sung at the same time? Is it pleasing, or harsh?

 **Science**

Aristotle is considered the Father of the Scientific Method. He emphasized:
- the importance of making one's own discoveries
- collecting information
- analyzing the information
- classifying the information

• Choose an animal or plant that you can find nearby. Observe your subject. Weigh it, measure it, poke it (if possible), smell it, test it every way you can think of. Write down everything you observe. Did you discover anything you didn't already know? What new ways could you classify the subject?

  Thales (thay-leez) was another Greek scientist and philosopher. He figured out how to measure the height of the Great Pyramid of Cheops, based on an observation. He knew his own height, and could measure the height of his shadow. He could also measure the height of the pyramid's shadow. With these three numbers known, it was possible to calculate the fourth unknown number (the height of the pyramid.)

• Try measuring a tall tree like this: On a sunny day, make a stake three and a half feet tall. Drive it into the ground so that it is three feet tall. Now measure the length of the stake's shadow. Measure the length of the tree's shadow. You can now figure the height of the tree! Just solve for **x**.

$$\frac{\text{Height of Stake}}{\text{Height of Stake Shadow}} = \frac{\text{Height of Tree (X)}}{\text{Height of Tree Shadow}}$$

 **Cooking**

  Greek foods are one of my absolute favorites! There are so many recipes to choose from, but this one is one of the best.

Baklava   Serves 8

10 sheets filo pastry (freezer section)	1/2 cup honey
1/2 cup melted butter	1/2 tsp. ground cloves
1 1/4 cup finely chopped walnuts	1/2 tsp. grated orange peel
1/4 cup honey	1 tsp. lemon juice
1/2 tsp. cinnamon	

Cut pastry sheets in half (20 12x8 inch sheets). Brush 7 sheets of filo with butter and layer them into a buttered 12x8 metal baking pan. Combine walnuts, 1/4 cup honey, and cinnamon. Spread 1/4 of the mixture over filo in pan. Cover with 2 more sheets of buttered filo, then add another 1/4 of the mixture. Repeat until you have used a total of 13 sheets of filo and all of the mixture. Brush remaining 7 sheets of filo with butter, and place on top of sheets in the pan. With a sharp knife, cut pastry to form 16 diamond-shaped pieces. Top with remaining butter and bake in 350 oven for about 50 minutes, until top is crisp. While baking, combine remaining ingredients in a small pan. Bring to a boil, then lower heat and simmer for 8 to 10 minutes. Remove baklava from oven. Top immediately with hot syrup. Cool.

Idea Time!

Creative Writing

- Write the annals of Aristotle's assistant, assigned to acquire all the animals for Aristotle's assessment.
- Compose a poem entitled, "To the Athenians and their Unknown God."
- Be a reporter visiting Sparta before the outbreak of the Peloponnesian wars. Describe the training, the tenseness, and the tenacity of the Spartans for the magazine, "The Modern Military."
- Discover the connection these words have to the unit, and then write a rhyming poem (or poems) using them:
    culture, sculpture, picture
    Pericles, Themistocles, Hippocrates
    Parthenon, Marathon, Xenophon

Art

- Draw a cartoon of the shortness & wonder of the Golden Age of Greece.

Drama

- Aristotle, Pericles, Pythagoras, Thales, Themistocles, and Alexander are all going to receive an award at a Greek banquet. You are the emcee for the banquet. Introduce at length each of these famous Greeks to explain why they merit this award.
- Perform the scene from Josephus about Alexander the Great coming to Jerusalem. Use your imagination for costumes, props, horses (!), etc.
- Do a humorous skit showing little Alex begging his father, King Philip, to let him ride that big black horse (Bucephalus.) Be sure to include the look of surprise on everyone's face while he is riding!

The Big Picture

- Consider what you have learned about Greece, about the prophecies of Alexander the Great, and about the perspective on the Greeks that Paul had in the Mars Hill sermon. How can you present this to your family, friends, neighbors, church? How can you convey the story of ancient Greece while adding the perspective of God's plan and involvement with these people? Remember, it is not enough to know about or even to appreciate an historic time. We must search to understand God's heart for the people in order to truly understand their culture. Pray for modern Greece: for the leaders, the people, the missionaries, the church.

Unit Ten

The Hellenistic Period -
Ptolemies, Seleucids, Maccabees

The Pharos of Alexandria

Unit Objectives:

- to understand the impact of the breakup of Alexander's empire;

- to consider the influence of the Greek worldview upon the Jews;

- to understand the historical reasons for Hanukkah;

- to learn about the Pharos of Alexandria, the Temple of Artemis, and the Colossus of Rhodes ;

- to see the remarkable achievements in math and science during this time period.

Meet the People

- **The Holy Bible**
  Read Daniel 8:8-12, 21-22; 11:4; Acts 19:1-41.

- **Apocrypha**
  1 Maccabees is one of the major historical accounts of the Maccabean revolt. It, along with Josephus, contains the best record of these events.   Good for family!

- **Josephus**
  Book XII, chapters V - VIII, contains the account of Antiochus Epiphanies and his desecration of the Temple in Jerusalem. The resulting rebellion on the part of the pious Jews was led first by Mattathias Maccabeus and then by his son Judas. It is an incredible tale of courage, of military shrewdness, and of God's blessing.   **Great read aloud!**

- **World Leaders Past and Present: Judas Maccabeus** by E. H. Fortier
  This is a riveting look at the Maccabean Revolt which occurred during the Hellenistic period. Skip Chapter Three, which deals with the history of Israel, because the author does not have a Biblical worldview. However, apart from that chapter, the book is fascinating, filled with historical details, and reads like fiction.   **Junior High and up.**

- **Mathematicians are People, Too** by Reimer and Reimer
  This book contains my favorite description of Archimedes (scientist, inventor, mathematician, and all around genius!) When we can learn about these people in their actual time period, it makes them interesting and memorable.   **Great read aloud!**

- **Make it Work! Ships** by Andrew Solway
  All of the books in this series are absolute wonders, especially because they truly create an environment for the whole family to discover science, history, etc. This book is great because it demonstrates the displacement of ships in water. That is the principle of buoyancy, which was discovered by Archimedes (see above book.)   **Great for the family!**

- **Make it Work! Machines** by David Glover
  One more experiment to show an invention of Archimedes. He invented the water screw, which still has many functions and is used in many parts of the world. A fabulous book!
                      Great for the family!

- Also read about the Ptolemies, Seleucids and Maccabeans in a study Bible, Bible handbook, or Bible dictionary. Though many history books skip this period of time, it is critical to understand the struggle taking place between the Hellenistic worldview and the Biblical worldview.

To follow the "Warfare and Weaponry" strand in ancient history, we recommend:

- **Warfare in the Classical World** by John Warry
  An absolutely incredible book for those interested in following world history through warfare and weaponry. This book contains the best timeline I've ever seen for ancient civilizations. It is certainly worth the search.   **Junior High and up.**

- **Charge! Weapons and Warfare in Ancient Times**
  Filled with pictures, this book also details ancient history through warfare. Excellent for the younger students interested in this aspect of history.   **Upper elem & up.**

- **Digging Up the Past: Weapons and Warfare** by Rivka Gonen
It's amazing how much we can learn about ancient cultures through their wars and weapons, both the winners and losers.   **Upper elem and up.**

- **Military History of the World - Volume One** by J.F.C. Fuller
For those who really want to dig into this subject, this is the book to get. We found it at a military college!   **High school and up.**

Talk Together

- Listen to What in the World's Going on Here?, Tape Two. What was the most interesting aspect to you of the events in the breakup of Alexander's empire which were mentioned? Why? What questions do you have about this time period that you would like to learn more about?
     History Journal: Write those questions down, and as you study more material, write the answers to your questions. Write short bios of the interesting people. Illustrate the bios.

- Why do you think that four generals were needed to take over Alexander's empire, rather than just one? What country were the generals from? Think about what you learned about the Greeks in the last unit. What did the Greeks think about "foreign" people? Who did the Greeks consider to be "barbarian"? Why? What opinion did the ruling generals have of foreigners in their lands?

- After reading about this time period in a Bible handbook or commentary, look at a map of the Middle East. Where were the Ptolemies located? Where were the Seleucids located? What country was in between? What was the result for the people living in between?

- About 270 B.C., the Pharos (or Lighthouse) of Alexandria was built. Why was it considered to be one of the ancient wonders of the world? The Great Wall of China was finished about 220 B.C. Why wasn't this amazing structure selected as one of the seven ancient wonders?

- This was a tremendous time of scientific and mathematical discoveries. Euclid wrote about geometry, Eratoshthenes measured the circumference of the world (very accurately!) and Archimedes discovered the principle of buoyancy, among other things. Why do you think this was such a time of discovery? What factors contributed to Archimedes' inventions and discoveries? (**Hint:** Necessity is the mother of invention.)

- Ptolemy II had the Old Testament translated from Hebrew to Greek. Why? What do you think the benefits were to the Jews? Why? Who else might have wanted to read the holy book of the Jews?

- Investigate Acts 19 in the New Testament. Why was Demetrius so upset? Describe the scene, Paul's part in it, and what the result was.

Teaching Time!

Seminar Outline

◇ X. Breakup of Alexander's Empire
◇   A) Ptolemies - Egypt
◇   B) Seleucids - Syria
◇   1) Antiochus Epiphanies, King
◇   2) Maccabean Revolt
◇   a) Mattathias
◇   b) Judas
◇   C) Antigonids - Macedonia
◇   D) Lysimachus - Thrace

Timeline

→ On your timeline, mark Ptolemy II and the Septuagint, Antiochus Epiphanies and the Maccabean Revolt, the first Hanukkah, Archimedes, Eratosthenes, Euclid, the Pharos of Alexandria, the Great Wall of China, the Colossus of Rhodes, the Temple of Artemis.

Research & Reporting:

• Find one of the books listed at the beginning of this unit, along with the encyclopedia or other history resource book for basic information on the Maccabean revolt.

• What was the short term result of Antiochus Epiphanies' desecration of the Temple? What was the long term result?

- Do a research paper with pictures on Hanukkah and its beginning.

- Research and report on the differences during the Hellenistic period between the Greeks and the Jews. (**Hint:** Find out about the forms of education, recreation, religion.)

- Research and report on the Ptolemies in regards to their treatment of the Jews. How did the Seleucids differ? Does your research indicate any reason for this difference?

- Look up and write about Alexandria as a center of learning and influence.

- Research and report on the "Rise and Fall of the Ptolemies and the Seleucids."

- Compile a list of names, dates and accomplishments of the key leaders of the Hellenistic period.

- In the library, or on the Internet, research any information related about Syria. (Newspapers, magazines, books, videos)

- Investigate the scientific and mathematical discoveries of Archimedes, Euclid and Eratosthenes. Report your findings.

- Find out more about the wonders of the ancient world that were built during the Hellenistic period. How long did they last? Were they still standing in New Testament times? Were they seen by any New Testament figures?

- Compare and contrast the events in the Middle East during this time with the events in China and India.

- Summarize the major events during this time period. Draw a chart to show these events, their location, dates and participants.

Vocabulary

circumference	Eratosthenes	geometry	Euclid
buoyancy	fulcrum	Archimedes	desecrate
guerrilla warfare	Judas Maccabeus	Ptolemy	Seleucid
library	Alexandria	translate	Hanukkah
Menorah	colossal	hellenize	Septuagint
assimilate			

Hands On!

Maps
and
Mapping

• Using an atlas, encyclopedia or other resource, locate Syria, Thrace, Macedonia, Sicily, and Alexandria on a map.

• What is the name of the country or countries that today occupy the same area as the above? What is the capital city, religion, population, major exports, and type of government in each modern country? What is the status of Christian outreach to these countries?

• On a clean worksheet map, draw the boundaries of Ptolemaic Egypt (including the conquests), Syria (including the conquests), and Israel. Label the location of Alexandria, Jerusalem, and other important cities. What modern day cities are close to these ancient cities?

• Consult a relief map to discover the terrain of Syria, as well as of Israel and Egypt. Is it desert, mountain, forest, swamp, coastal? What type of climate is typical in that part of the world? How would the terrain and climate have affected God's purposes as seen in the Maccabean revolt?

 Arts in Action

The Festival of Hanukkah is also known as the Festival of Lights.

• To illustrate this, try making your own candles. Since melted wax can be dangerous (it is VERY hot!), adult supervision is required. Consult your library or local expert for more info.

• After they are made, light one in a dark room. Then read John 8:12.

- Trace a picture of a war elephant. They were considered to be a vital part of the military maneuvers of that time period.

- Make a model of the Pharos Lighthouse of Alexandria. Legos would be a great building material, or papier maché, or modeling clay. Try setting up the Pharos on a harbor of blue construction paper, showing that the lighthouse was on an island and that Alexandria was on the mainland.

Art Appreciation

- If possible, locate artists' renditions of:

  Pharos of Alexandria

  Temple of Artemis

  The Colossus of Rhodes

- What can we learn about the technical and creative ability of the people of this time period?

 Music

The Maccabean revolt shows how many Jews resisted assimilation into the Greek worldview and culture. One way a people group maintains its unique identity is through its music.

Have you ever listened to Jewish music? There is a certain flavor, a certain style which sets it apart from other ethnic music. We enjoy singing Jewish songs (including worship choruses) around our house and even dancing the "hora."

- Listen to some selections of Jewish music. "Fiddler on the Roof" contains marvelous music with lots of humor. Itzak Perlman, one of the top violinists in the world, has recorded some Israeli music that is worth listening to. The Judeo-Christian group, "Lamb", sings beautiful music with a definite Jewish flair. If you look around, you will surely find something that qualifies.

- **Try this:** Learn some lively Jewish worship choruses, and then find someone to teach you to dance the hora. If you are out of shape, prepare yourself! This is extraordinarily fun and intensely aerobic!

Science

- Experiment with the principle of buoyancy. You could try Archimedes' experiment by getting into the bath tub and seeing how high the water rises. If you are really adventurous, set a full tub on a big sheet of plastic out in the yard, and see how much water spills out when you get in! Or, try dropping various materials of different weights into a jar of water. Record the different levels the water rises to. Do larger items displace more water? Do heavier items displace more water than larger items?

- If possible, try the experiment on Archimedes' screw in **Make it Work! Machines**. (See **Resource List** for ordering info.)

Cooking

Celebrate the miracle of Hanukkah with lots of oil! It is traditional to eat both potato cakes and fried doughnuts. (Thankfully, this feasting is not for every day!) Afterwards, taste the goodness of Syrian cooking with lentil and tomatoes.

Potato Latkes

4 large potatoes (peeled, grated)   2 Tbsp. flour
1 small onion (grated)   salt & pepper
3 eggs (beaten)

Drop by large spoonfuls into a hot, oiled fry pan. Cook until brown on both sides. Serve warm and topped with sour cream, applesauce or yogurt.

Lentils with tomatoes   Serves 4

1 cup brown lentils   1 tsp ground cumin
1/4 cup oil   1/2 cup beef bouillon
1 large onion, minced   4 tomatoes, peeled and chopped
2 cloves garlic, minced   Salt & pepper

Soak lentils in cold water for 3 hours. Discard any floating lentils, drain. Place lentils in pot of rapidly boiling salted water and cook over medium heat 30 min. Drain, reserve. Heat oil in large saucepan. Add onions and garlic, sauté about 5 minutes. Stirring constantly, add cumin and cook over high heat for 2 minutes. Add bouillon and lentils. Mix thoroughly, then simmer, uncovered, over low heat until lentils are almost tender (15 minutes.) Stir in tomatoes and season. Continue simmering until tomatoes are tender, about 15 minutes. Serve immediately.

Idea Time!

Creative Writing

- Write a first person account about translating the Old Testament into Greek, along with your other Jewish scholar friends in Alexandria.

- Be a war correspondent for the "Voice of the Maccabeans" and write the behind-the-scenes story of Judas Maccabeus and his guerrilla army.

- Compose a poem about the Festival of Lights (Hanukkah).

- As a sailor, describe the Pharos of Alexandria to folks at home who have never seen it.

- Imagine you are the city clerk at Ephesus in Acts 19. Write a report of the day's events for the city record.

Art

- Illustrate a book for young children showing the history of Hanukkah, and how it is celebrated today.

Drama

- Act out the scene in the Temple when the Menorah was kept miraculously lit. Use your imagination to create props, sets and costumes. Be sure to include realistic rejoicing!

- Create a scene showing Eratosthenes figuring out how to measure the world. Be sure to include some of the principles he used.

- Do a humorous skit about Archimedes' discovery of buoyancy.

The Big Picture

- Celebrate the Festival of Lights. Look up all the different aspects of the celebration: food, games, gifts, lights. Come up with a plan to share with your family, church, support group, school, or neighbors this amazing period of history, and how God preserved His people in the midst of terrible persecution. Rejoice in the grace and goodness of God!

Unit Eleven

The Rise of Rome

The Colosseum

Unit Objectives:

- to understand the rise of Rome and the significance of the Empire;

- to learn about Julius Caesar, Mark Antony and Octavian and the part they each played in world history;

- to become familiar with the remarkable engineering feats of the Romans;

- to see God's sovereign hand in using this Empire to accomplish His plan of redemption.

 *Meet the People*

- **The Holy Bible**
  Read   Daniel 2:33-35,40-45; Luke 2:1-3.

- **Caesar's Gallic War** translated, edited by Olivia Coolidge
  This version of Julius Caesar's autobiographical account of the Gallic War is fabulous! Olivia Coolidge has added enough "color" that it draws the reader in to the story. I absolutely recommend it! **Junior High and up.**

- **Hannibal's Elephants** by Alfred Powers
  A fictionalized account of the mighty Hannibal, general of Carthage. It is told from the perspective of a boy who helps care for the war elephants during the Second Punic War with Rome. It is very interesting, especially for boys. **Upper elem and up.**

- **Plutarch - Lives of Noble Romans** edited by Fuller
  Plutarch was one of the earliest biographers in history! All the plays William Shakespeare wrote about the Romans were derived from Plutarch's biographies. Difficult reading, but some may enjoy it. Plutarch compared Roman leaders with Greek leaders.
  High school and up.

- **"Julius Caesar"** by William Shakespeare

- **Lives of Famous Romans** by Olivia Coolidge
  Any set of biographies on the Romans is bound to be distasteful to some extent, since so many of the ruling Romans (especially of the Empire) were given over to utter immorality. My suggestion is to read these biographies in light of Daniel 2, and the perspective given in the gospels and Acts. **High school and up.**

- **Famous Men of Rome** edited by Rob Shearer
  A much gentler version of the above book, it gives a good introduction to the most important men of this empire. **Elementary and up.**

- **Augustus Caesar's World** by Genevieve Foster
  A fascinating book for all ages which tells the story of Augustus Caesar, describing the world in which he lived. Though it has been out of print for a time, it should be back in print soon.
  Elementary and up.

- **Growing Up in Ancient Rome** by Mike Corbishley
  Another book in the series, this is one of the best books I know for introducing the lifestyle and culture of ancient Rome. Excellent overview for children. **Elementary and up.**

- **World Leaders Past and Present: Julius Caesar** by Roger Bruns
  An excellent book in this excellent series! I preferred this book to the one about Mark Antony, and much of the same time period and material is covered. After reading Caesar's Gallic Wars, this book will fill in the gaps. **Junior High and up.**

- **World Leaders Past and Present: Cleopatra** by Hoobler and Hoobler
This book takes a sympathetic look at the last reigning Ptolemy in Egypt. Cleopatra was revered by the Egyptians, loved by Caesar and Antony, and hated by the Romans. Learn why in this intriguing book. **Junior High and up.**

- **City** by David Macauley
Mr. Macauley helps us to see the incredible cultural dynamic of architecture. Learn how a Roman city was designed and built in this fascinating book.
Good for the family!

- **The Lost Wreck of the Isis** by Robert D. Ballard
Learn about underwater archaeology while reading a fictional tale of a ship lost at sea during Roman times. Very interesting. **Upper elem and up.**

- **Sunk! Exploring Underwater Archaeology**
This is a fascinating book showing how archaeologists discover new aspects of history and ancient cultures under the water. **Upper elem and up.**

- **Bridges: A Project Book** by Anne & Scott MacGregor
If you can find the book, there is a wonderful project for building a Roman-arch bridge.
Projects for family!

- **Piece by Piece! Mosaics of the Ancient World**
A wonderful look at this art form, this book is filled with pictures and the stories mosaics have "told" to archaeologists. **Elementary and up.**

- **Make it Work! Building** by David Glover
Another book from this fantastic series, this one shows two different projects for the family to do: a keystone bridge and an aqueduct. See the Resource List for ordering info.
Projects for family!

- **Make it Work! The Roman Empire** by Peter Chrisp
This is a hands-on approach to learning history! Filled with ideas for Roman clothing, art, architecture, weaponry, and more, it certainly has enough ideas to keep everyone happy. See the Resource List for ordering info. **Projects for family!**

Talk Together

- Listen to What in the World's Going on Here? Tape Two. What was the most interesting aspect to you of the events in the rise of Rome which were mentioned? Why? What questions do you have about this time period that you would like to learn more about?
  History Journal: Write those questions down, and as you study more material, write the answers to your questions. Write short bios of the interesting people. Illustrate the bios.

- Why do you think the Punic Wars were important in the history of Rome?

- Imagine you were with Hannibal as he crossed the Alps with his army and elephants. Describe to your family the trip through the mountains and the effectiveness of the elephants against the surprised Romans.

- After looking at a map of the Roman Empire, consider the natural boundaries and how they were enlarged significantly by conquering other lands. What words would you use to describe this empire?

- Why do you think Jesus came and began His Church during the Roman Empire? What did the Romans bring to the world that may have enhanced the spread of Christianity?

- What can you discover about this culture in regards to their treatment of other peoples? Were they similar to the Assyrians, Babylonians, Persians or Greeks? In what ways? How were they different?

- How did the Roman Republic differ from the Roman Empire? What factors led to the Empire? Imagine you are a citizen of Rome living during the Empire. Tell how, according to your parents, things have changed from the time of the Republic.

- What is the significance of the Ides of March? What historic event took place on that date? How might history have been different if this event had not occurred?

- Cleopatra had an important role in this time period. Some biographers describe her as a shrewd political leader trying to hold onto her power in a tumultuous time, doing only what was necessary to save her throne. Others describe her as a bewitching woman with almost magical powers over men. How would you evaluate her actions in light of the Scriptures? Read Proverbs 14:12. How does this proverb help you interpret the life of Cleopatra?

- Towards the end of the Roman Republic there was the first **triumvirate**, or council of three men, who led Rome. Who were the three leaders and what was the result of that triumvirate? After Julius Caesar's death there was another triumvirate. Who were the three leaders, and what resulted from their union?

- The Romans created amazing bridges, aqueducts and roads which still exist in many places. Why do you suppose they put so much effort into building them? What purpose did these engineering marvels fulfill?

- Imagine you were a Roman soldier traveling to Gaul with Julius Caesar. What are some terms you could use to describe life as a Roman soldier?

- Describe the climate and terrain of Rome. What kind of crops were grown? What kind of animals were raised? How were the large cities (like Rome) supplied with food, clothing and other goods? What impact did the conquests have on the people back in Rome?

- Who were the slaves in Rome? How did the Romans acquire their slaves?

- Can you see any Greek influence in the Roman civilization? (**Hint:** Look at their religion.) Why do you think the Romans were impressed with Greek culture? What was the impact of this Greco-Roman culture on the Jews in Palestine?

Teaching Time!

Seminar Outline

◇ XI. Rise of Rome
◇　　　　A) Republic
◇　　　　　　1) Punic Wars against Carthage from 264-146 B.C.
◇　　　　　　　　a) Built their navy
◇　　　　　　　　b) Hannibal of Carthage
◇　　　　　　　　　　1) crossed Alps in 15 days with 50,000 men
◇ `　　　　　　　　　2) 38 elephants
◇　　　　　　　　c) Scipio, General of Rome
◇　　　　B) End of Republic - personal peace and prosperity instead of freedom
◇　　　　　　1) Julius Caesar, Conqueror
◇　　　　　　　　a) Cleopatra, Queen of Egypt (last of the Ptolemies)
◇　　　　　　　　b) Assassinated
◇　　　　　　2) Mark Antony, Caesar's General
◇　　　　　　　　a) Triumvirate
◇　　　　　　　　b) Cleopatra
◇　　　　C) Empire
◇　　　　　　1) Octavian - the schoolboy
◇　　　　　　　　a) Triumvirate
　　　　　　　　　b) Battle of Actium
　　2) Augustus Caesar - First Roman Emperor

Timeline

→　On your timeline, mark the Etruscans, Romulus and Remus, the Punic Wars, Hannibal, Scipio, Julius Caesar, Cleopatra, Mark Antony, Augustus Caesar, Roman Republic, Roman Empire.

Research & Reporting:

- Find one of the books listed at the beginning of this unit, along with the encyclopedia or other history resource book for basic information on Rome - first, the Republic and then, the Empire.

- On a map, locate Carthage, Rome, and the Alps. Research and write a detailed description of Hannibal's surprise route. What was the short term result of the Punic Wars? What was the long term result for Carthage? Rome?

- Discover the changes made in the calendar by Julius Caesar.

- Research and report on the "Rise and Fall of the Roman Republic."

- Find out about the use of navies in warfare during this time period. Research and report on the Battle of Actium.

- Look up Julius Caesar in your history resources. How significant was this leader in Roman history? What is the significance of the Rubicon River in his life? How was the Republic affected by his death?

- Research and report your comparisons of the first Triumvirate with the second Triumvirate.

- In the library, or on the Internet, investigate the history of Rome (Italy) from the time of the Republic to the present. Report your findings as if you were a newspaper reporter. (Journalism)

- Discover the methods used by the Romans to build roads. Draw a diagram showing the different steps used. Arches had been used in architectural design for centuries, but the Romans found a better design and use for the arch. Discover what made the Roman arched bridges and aqueducts so strong that several remain even two thousand years later.

- The Romans had been described in the book of Daniel hundreds of years before they emerged as world leaders. Using a study Bible, Bible handbook, Bible dictionary, commentary, etc., research the possible reasons God intended Jesus to come during this empire. What set this empire apart from earlier ones?

Vocabulary

republic	Pax Romana	triumvirate
Punic Wars	Carthage	Hannibal
aqueduct	Julius Caesar	Cleopatra
Mark Antony	emperor	slave
Octavian	tribune	centurion
legion	senate	patricians
empire	plebians	

Hands On!

**Maps
and
Mapping**

- Using an atlas, encyclopedia or other resource, locate the Roman Empire on a map.

- What is the name of the country or countries that today occupy the same area as the Roman Empire? What is the capital city, religion, population, major exports, and type of government in each modern country? What is the status of Christian outreach to these countries?

- On a clean worksheet map, draw the boundaries of Rome (including the conquests in the Republic and Empire). Label the location of Carthage and Rome. Locate the sites where Roman governors commanded. What modern day cities are close to these ancient cities?

- Consult a relief map to discover the terrain of Rome. Was it desert, mountain, forest, swamp, coastal? What type of climate is typical in that part of the world? How would the terrain and climate have affected the Roman culture and God's purpose for it?

 Arts in Action

- Make Roman costumes. The library will have books to show you how.

- Try making an artistic mosaic. There are many ways to do this, from very simple to very complicated. One wonderful idea is to create a papier maché bowl, paint it a base color, then create a pattern inside the bowl with colored bits of paper. Complete your masterpiece by giving a coat of varnish, inside and out.

- Carve an elephant out of soap. Start with the trunk, round the head, shoulders, then carefully carve the legs. (Just carve away everything that doesn't look like elephant!)

- Get a big cardboard box. Paint the Swiss Alps on the inside back and sides. Using miniature figures, create a diorama of Hannibal crossing the Alps with his army, horses and elephants.

Art Appreciation

- Look up pictures of the mosaics from Pompeii, statues of famous Romans, the Colosseum of Rome and the aqueduct in Nimes, France.

Who did the Romans imitate in their art and architecture?

 ## Music

The Romans developed many brass instruments used in military music. For example, the Roman straight trumpet (they called a tuba) was like the herald trumpet used today at horse races. Another was the buccina, which had a wooden crossbar to allow soldiers to carry it on the march. These instruments were very simple in structure and so they had very limited range of pitches. Their purpose was not to entertain people, but for signaling. They could call the soldiers to assemble, or they could signal the soldiers to move.

It wasn't until centuries later that further developments allowed these instruments to have more melodic ability, thereby allowing them to come inside! Now, of course, it is very common to see trumpets and tubas, etc., in orchestras and bands. But there is still a certain thrill in hearing them played outdoors at concerts and celebrations.

- Listen to some of John Phillip Sousa's march music, such as "Stars and Stripes Forever" or the "Washington Post March." (You might want to march with them!)

- **Try this:** Cut the bottoms off plastic pop (soda) bottles. A 2-liter bottle gives a lower sound, while a 16 oz. bottle gives a higher sound. Now, play it like a trumpet: tighten your lips, center the mouth of the bottle over both lips, blow air through a small opening between your lips very fast - fast enough so your lips will buzz. This buzzing will make sound come out of the bottle. If you tighten your lips more and blow faster air, the pitch will go up. If you loosen your lips and blow slower, the pitch will go down. Try placing your fist in the bottom of the "tuba" - it will give a nice variation. Your pop bottle "tuba" will sound somewhat like those early instruments, in that they weren't very pretty either!

Science

- Make an arched bridge. We found books in the library (listed at the beginning of the unit) which gave detailed descriptions of how to do this. Be sure and learn what a keystone is, how it functions and why it is important.

- Make an aqueduct. An incredible "build-it-together" example is found in the Make it Work! Buildings book. (See resource list for ordering info.)

Cooking

The Romans were extremely fond of an herb we usually use in licorice - anise. It was considered to be so delightful that kings perfumed their linen with it. (Imagine sleeping on a pillow that smelled like licorice!) This recipe is **not** from Roman times, but it is a delicious way to sample this favored herb.

Anise Cookies

4 eggs
1 cup sugar
1 tsp vanilla
1/3 cup milk

2 tbsp anise seed
3 cups flour
4 tsp baking powder
1 cup butter, softened

Preheat oven to 375 degrees. Beat eggs well in large bowl. Add sugar, vanilla, milk, and anise. Stir well. In another bowl, mix flour and baking powder. Cut in butter. Combine 2 mixtures. Roll dough out onto floured board. Cut into shapes. Bake on greased baking sheet 12 minutes, or until lightly browned.

Makes about 4 dozen.

Idea Time!

Creative Writing

- Write a fictional account of Remus, the Roman road builder (no relation to the Roman Republic builder.) Of the 53,000 miles of road built by Rome, Remus has been told to build from Rome to Rhegium.
- Be the newspaper reporter assigned to cover Octavian's triumphal entry into Rome after defeating Mark Antony and Cleopatra. Be sure to include the background information about Julius Caesar's will which promoted Octavian to power.
- Make your own version of Timetables of History showing what is taking place in the arts, in science, in math, in family life, and in government during the rise of Rome.
- Create a crossword puzzle. Choose words from this unit for the horizontal and vertical answers. Next, supply the clues which will enable your family to solve the puzzle.

Art

- As a political cartoonist, show the attitude of the Roman women toward Cleopatra.
- Illustrate a short story about a reluctant elephant on the march with Hannibal. Call it "The Bashful Behemoth."

Drama

- Act out the angels listening to Augustus Caesar's proclamation to register all the people in the Empire. Caesar is trying to make up his mind how and when he wants this done. The angels know the prophecies, so they are very excited when he finally makes a decision. They all get in line to volunteer for messenger duty to the shepherds! Use your imagination to create props, sets and costumes.

The Big Picture

- How can you present what you've learned about the rise of Rome and the Bible? Remember to show how God prepared for the arrival of the Messiah. Come up with a plan to share with your family, church, support group, school, or neighbors this exciting look at God's grace in bringing to pass the "fullness of time." Galatians 4: 4 - 5.

Unit Twelve

Jesus Christ, Messiah

The Last Supper

Unit Objectives:

- to understand the fullness of time in God's plan;

- to know Him, and the power of His resurrection, and the fellowship of His sufferings; Philippians 3:10

- to comprehend with all the saints what is the width and length and depth and height - to know the love of Christ which passes knowledge; that you may be filled with all the fullness of God;
  Ephesians 3:17-19

- to learn the historical setting and the historical evidence for the birth, life, death and resurrection of Jesus the Christ;

- to be able to share knowledgeably and compassionately about these things with those who do not know Jesus as their Messiah.

Meet the People

- **The Holy Bible**
  Read Isaiah 46:9-10, Romans 1:2-4, Genesis 3:15, Isaiah 7:14, Psalm 2:7, Genesis 22:18, Numbers 24:17, Genesis 49:10, Isaiah 11:1, Jeremiah 23:5, Micah 5:2, Jeremiah 31:15, Psalm 110:1 & 4, Deuteronomy 18:18, Isaiah 33:22, Isaiah 61:1-3, Psalm 69:9, Isaiah 40:3, Isaiah 9:1, Isaiah 35:5-6, Psalm 78:2, Malachi 3:1, Zechariah 9:9, Psalm 118:22, Isaiah 60:3, Psalm 16:10, Psalm 41:9, Zechariah 11:12-13, Zechariah 13:7, Psalm 35:11, Isaiah 53, Isaiah 50:6, Psalm 22, Psalm 109:24-25, Psalm 69:4 & 21, Psalm 38:11, Psalm 31:5, Psalm 34:20, Zechariah 12:10, Amos 8:9, Matthew, Mark, Luke, John, Acts.

- **Evidence that Demands a Verdict** by Josh McDowell
  This is not a book to sit down and read, it is a book to study. It will teach you the historical evidences for the Christian faith (a term often used for this is "apologetics"). Filled with historical, archaeological, medical, legal references, this book will give you and your students a very firm foundation for the defense of Biblical Christianity. **Junior High and up. (Though the whole family could benefit from studying together)**

- **Pontius Pilate** by Paul Maier
  Historical fiction, the events of this book are based entirely on historic documentation. It is a fascinating look at this historic person. (There is one scene I would avoid, when Salome dances for King Herod.) **Junior High and up.**

- **The Bronze Bow** by Elizabeth Speare
  Written for children, this is an absorbing tale about a young Jewish boy who struggles with his hatred for the conquering Romans. A very good insight into the mood of the times. **Elementary and up.**

- **Ben Hur** by Lew Wallace
  This classic is written from the perspective of a prince of Judah who is thrown into Roman slavery. When he regains his freedom, he joins the guerrilla fighters who want a political Messiah. Having watched the movie and also read the book, I would highly recommend the book as it contains far more understanding of the culture, the times, the thoughts of the people. **Junior High and up.**

- **Ben Hur** edited by Kottmeyer
  If reading the original is beyond your students, you may want to consider getting a younger version. **Elementary and up.**

- **The Runaway** by Patricia St. John
  A very good story about a Phoenician boy whose sister is demon-possessed. The Scriptures come to life as you see the boy encounter many different people who have met Jesus. Our family couldn't put it down! **Good read aloud!**

- **Vinegar Boy** by Alberta Hawse
  This is the story of the boy assigned to bring vinegar to those who were crucified. It is a story of the bitterness of defeat being turned into the joy of victory **Upper elem and up.**

- **The Robe** by Lloyd Douglas
  This is an excellent look at Roman ways and their conflict with Christianity. **Junior High-up.**

Talk Together

- Listen to What in the World's Going on Here?, Tape Two. What was the most interesting aspect to you of the events surrounding the coming of Jesus, the Messiah, which were mentioned? Why? What questions do you have about this time period that you would like to learn more about?

    History Journal: Write those questions down, and as you study more material, write the answers to your questions. Write short bios of the interesting people. Illustrate the bios.

- Why do you think God sent Jesus to be born of peasants rather than kings?

- Imagine you are one of the shepherds who had heard the angelic announcement. Describe your surprise, your amazement and your awe at actually seeing the Christ child.

- Read the prophecies of the Messiah in the Old Testament (listed in the Bible readings). How are they each fulfilled in the birth, life, death, or resurrection of Jesus?

- After answering the above question, discuss with your family how you could share what you have learned with one who believes Jesus was merely a man.

- Read the book of Mark. It clearly reveals the miraculous power of Jesus to heal the sick, calm the storm, cast out demons, feed the multitude, die a sacrificial death and rise from the dead unto eternal life. What would someone who believes in a "closed system" - does not believe in God and does not believe in the supernatural - say about these miracles? Why?

- What is the difference between a person who says, "I don't know, but let's do some research to find out" and the person who says, "I already know it isn't true"? Why will the second person not believe any historic evidence for the truth of Christianity? What will help them believe? (**Hint:** Love!)

- The amazing thing about studying Jesus is that He is ALIVE! When we studied Moses, King Nebuchadnezzar, Xerxes, Alexander the Great, and Julius Caesar, we studied about important men who had accomplished much during their lifetimes. But they are all dead. When we study Jesus, He is with us, revealing Himself, changing us, making us into His image. Take some time, either alone or with your family, to talk to Jesus about what you are studying. Ask Him your questions, bring Him your thoughts, allow Him to show you how He is the same, yesterday, today and forever.

- Read Matthew 11:28-30. What does Jesus tell us to do? Why? How do we obey Him? How will this change our lives?

- Ask the Lord to draw you into a closer walk with Him every day, to reveal His infinite love in your life. Keep an ongoing journal to show how this prayer is answered.

Teaching Time!

Seminar Outline

◇ XII. The Fullness of Time (Galatians 4:4-5)
◇   A) Rulers
◇   1) Augustus Caesar
◇   a) First Emperor of the Roman Empire
◇   b) Unlikely victor over Mark Antony
◇   2) Herod the Great
◇   a) Put in power by Mark Antony
◇   b) Architecturally, rebuilt the Temple
◇   1) Great in building projects
◇   2) Not great in relationships
◇   c) Caesar said, "I'd rather be Herod's pig than his son"
◇   d) Questioned the three Wise Men
◇   e) Slaughtered the young children
◇   B) Palestine
◇   1) Luke 2:1 - A decree went out from Caesar Augustus...
◇   a) Everyone to return to their family hometown
◇   b) Joseph and Mary had to travel to Bethlehem
◇   2) Jews under the yoke of Roman domination
◇   a) Roman soldiers stationed in Palestine
◇   b) Zealots want military overthrow
◇   C) God's Perfect Plan, Perfect Time, Perfect Son
◇   1) Jesus Christ, the Messiah
◇   2) God's Centerpiece of Human History

Timeline

→   On your timeline, mark the birth, life, death and resurrection of Jesus the Christ, Tiberius Caesar, Pontius Pilate, Herod Agrippa, Herod the Great.

Research & Reporting:

- Using either a Bible handbook, study Bible, commentary or **Evidence that Demands a Verdict**, make a chart showing the Old Testament prophecies of the Messiah, the date they were written, and the fulfillment of these prophecies in Jesus.

- Read the Gospels in the New Testament. To whom did Jesus come? What was His message? How did the people respond? How did the Resurrection impact the rulers of Jerusalem; of Rome? How did it impact the disciples?

- Research the mathematical probabilities that one man could fulfill all the prophecies of the Messiah.

- **Apologetics** is basically the intellectual defense of Christianity. Research and report on one area of apologetics, such as, fulfilled prophecy, evidence for the resurrection, the uniqueness and reliability of the Bible, etc.

- In reference books, research what was happening in the Roman Empire during the time of Jesus' life. Find the poem, "One Solitary Life," and show how it is historically accurate.

- Research and write about the claims of Jesus Christ. Who did He say He was? What did He claim to be able to do? What evidence exists to validate His claims? (**Hint:** I highly recommend investing in a copy of **Evidence That Demands a Verdict** or something similar. It will open up a whole world in understanding the reasonableness of our faith.)

- Make a chart showing the supernatural - outside of natural law - acts of Jesus. What did He do? What were the results of these miracles, both in the lives of those receiving the miracles and in the attitude of those watching Jesus do the miracles? In what ways do you see the same attitudes in people today?

- C.S. Lewis in Mere Christianity wrote: "I am trying here to prevent anyone saying the really foolish thing that people often say about Him: 'I'm ready to accept Jesus as a great moral teacher, but I don't accept His claim to be God.' That is the one thing we must not say. A man who was merely a man and said the sort of things Jesus said would not be a great moral teacher. He would either be a lunatic - on a level with the man who says he is a poached egg - or else he would be the Devil of Hell. You must make your choice. Either this man was, and is, the Son of God: or else a madman or something worse."
Write your response to this.

Vocabulary

natural	supernatural	miracle	hoax
myth	history	validate	Lord
Messiah	Emmanuel	Christ	disciple
apostle	resurrection	ascension	commission
crucify	tomb	swoon	proof/theory

Hands On!

Maps and Mapping

- Using an atlas, encyclopedia or other resource, locate Israel on a map.

- What is the name of the country or countries that today occupy the same area as ancient Israel? What is the capital city, religion, population, major exports, and type of government in each modern country? What is the status of Christian outreach to these countries?

- On a clean worksheet map, draw the boundaries of Israel. Label the location of Bethlehem, Nazareth, the Sea of Galilee, the Jordan river, the Decapolis, Samaria and all of the other geographical names given in the Gospels. What modern day cities are close to these ancient places?

- Consult a relief map to discover the terrain of Israel. Was it desert, mountain, forest, swamp, coastal? What type of climate is typical in that part of the world? How would the terrain and climate have affected the Jews and God's purpose for them?

Arts in Action

- Build a creche for a Nativity scene. This would be a great present to give your mother! If you can, find a craft book to show how to make bread dough figurines which can be painted. Or, it may be possible to buy greenware, clean it, paint it, and have it fired in a kiln. Ask a local ceramics or crafts expert how to do it.

- Sew a Passover lamb out of fleecy acrylic. Check in the library for the how-to information. Remember, the Passover lamb had to be without spot or blemish!

- Create a miniature Resurrection Day scene with bread dough, clay, or papier maché. Form it, paint it, add figures. The most important element is the Empty Tomb!

Art Appreciation

• If possible, find these paintings:
  The Annunciation
    by Jan Van Eyck
  Christ in the Storm on the Sea of Galilee
    by Rembrandt
  The Last Supper
    by Leonardo da Vinci
  Adoration of the Lamb
    by Jan Van Eyck

• And this sculpture:
  The Pieta
    by Michelangelo

Do these works of art reflect what the Bible describes?
How do they differ from your own impression of these historic events?
After observing these works of art, try to draw or paint these same scenes:
  1) imitating the artist (trace, follow colors, etc.)
  2) creating your own picture

 ## Music

"By faith we understand that the worlds were framed by the Word of God."
Hebrews 11:3

Have you ever noticed the remarkable structure evident in the universe? Rain falls, the moisture waters the earth, the water evaporates, the evaporation forms clouds, and the clouds produce rain. Everything that God created has structure and form, even if it is invisible to us.

In music, there is also a structure, a form. **Form** is the fifth element of music, and it is what holds all of the rest together. Without form there would not be familiar songs. There would only be random high notes and short notes and loud notes and low notes and fast notes and slow notes without any order. Does this sound somewhat like an evolutionary worldview - meaningless, chance and chaos? Actually, there are 20th century composers whose music reflects this worldview.

However, Colossians 1:16-17 states:
  "For by Him all things were created that are in heaven and that are on earth, visible and invisible... All things were created through Him and for Him. And He is before all things, and in Him all things are held together."   And Paul wrote in I Corinthians 14:40 that "all things should be done decently and in order."

To reflect the Biblical worldview, our music will have some form, some structure, some purpose. Handel's **"Messiah"** is a wonderful piece of musical literature about Jesus the Messiah. It incorporates many Old Testament prophecies in a rich setting of voices.

"The Messiah" is an **oratorio,** which means that it has a special form:

| I N C L U D E | - a long text, usually religious
- performed in a church or theater
- emphasis on chorus, with solos
- accompanied by orchestra | E X C L U D E | - rapid dialogue between characters
- scenery, costumes, and action
- emphasis on solos, with chorus
- very long sections |

The form of the oratorio is what distinguishes it from operas, symphonies, or choir concerts.

- Listen to these different pieces of music: Handel's "Messiah", an opera such as Mozart's "The Marriage of Figaro" and a symphony such as Haydn's "Surprise Symphony." Notice the differences in form, or structure, between these types of music. Name the differences you hear.

- **Try this:** After the above listening exercise, play "drop the needle" (which is an old-fashioned name since the advent of CD's!) One person will be the maestro and will secretly choose a recording, which the others will listen to. Play the recording at some randomly chosen spot and see who can identify the form of music being played.
Variation: Select any three different kinds of music for the maestro to choose from, such as country, jazz, and gospel. Can anyone in your family identify the form of music being played?

Science

- Jesus said, "A little leaven leavens the whole lump." Leaven is another term for yeast. Learn the meaning of Jesus' words by making a loaf of bread from scratch. How much yeast do you use in comparison to flour? What happens if the water is too hot? What if the water is too cold?

- 2 Corinthians 2:14 says "...and through us diffuses the fragrance of His knowledge in every place." Experiment with diffusion. Borrow a bottle of perfume from your mother. Set the closed bottle on a table. Does it smell? Now, hold your breath and spray the perfume in the air. Quickly step out of the room, and then return, breathing deeply. Can you smell the perfume? Try setting a bowl of potpourri in the kitchen. Can you smell it throughout the house? Now try heating the potpourri. Can you smell it throughout the house? Why? What can we learn about our life in Christ from this experiment?

Cooking

The fish was chosen to be one of the earliest Christian symbols. Taste & see!

Stuffed Baked Whitefish

3 cups bread cubes	3 tbsp water
1/4 cup melted butter	1/2 tsp salt
3/4 cup chopped cucumber	1/8 tsp freshly ground pepper
1/4 cup chopped onion	3 pounds whitefish, cleaned and boned

Combine the first seven ingredients and toss to mix well. Place stuffing lightly in fish cavity. Place in a greased baking pan; brush with oil. Bake in 375 oven for 30 min. or until fish flakes easily. Baste occasionally with oil. Serves 6.

Idea Time!

Creative Writing

- Write out the flow of history from Creation up to this moment in time. Show how Daniel's vision has been fulfilled through the four great empires. Galatians 4:4-5 indicates that God chose the perfect moment for the Messiah. In hind sight, how can we demonstrate that this was the case?
- Write a short story of the birth of Jesus from the perspective of the donkey who carried His mother to Bethlehem.
- Compose a song about how Jesus called fishermen to be fishers of men, and then gave them the power to preach.
- Be a newspaper reporter for "The Temple Times" investigating the incredible story of the empty tomb! You should include the background information that leads to this event.

Art

- Design a timeline for young children showing Jesus Christ as the Centerpiece of all of human history. You will be able to complete this as you study further in history.

Drama

- Act out the morning of the Resurrection. Use your imagination to create props, sets and costumes. Be sure to include realistic mourning and, then, rejoicing!
- Choose some scenes from the miracles of Jesus to pantomime. Find some appropriate recorded music (or have someone in your family perform) while these miracles are acted out.
- Do a humorous skit about the sower who went out to sow his seed. Be sure to include birds, hot sun, shallow roots, weeds, and fruitful plants.
- Role play a conversation using apologetics to explain the historical foundation of Christianity to a non-believing friend.

The Big Picture

- Plan a final presentation of what you have learned in this unit. How can you communicate with your family, friends, neighbors, church, support group, etc., what God did by sending His son, Jesus, in the fullness of time? How can you show the historical evidences for the Christian faith? How can you share the amazing love of God with others? Please write and let us know what your project was.